D1384184

Snow by Hélène Holden

ISBN 0 88750 819 7 (hardcover)
ISBN 0 88750 820 0 (softcover)

Cover photograph by Allan Eaton
Book design by Michael Macklem

Printed in Canada

PUBLISHED IN CANADA BY OBERON PRESS

For my brother, Basil

Sometimes, the Jack of Hearts felt a twinge of—not guilt, exactly, but how could Lois be doing that to them, and how could he let her? Such scruples of course only materialized at night. In the daytime, at the office, working alongside her husband who drove him up the wall with his nit-picking, Jack relapsed. He repositioned his head on her copious breasts, as it were, trying to imagine whether it would sink in there as on a down pillow, or bounce back, like on Qualofill—Madonna. How old was Lois anyway?

What? Boris said.

I was just thinking, Jack said, I've got to buy more pillows, my brother's coming over from Italy.

The prick, Boris thought. As if we could afford to tune off during office hours to worry about pillows. No substance to that man. No conscience. And my wife would dump me in a minute for a zero like that.

But Claribel would have told Boris what any fortune-teller knew: that there were just two kinds of women, the cheaters and the cheated. Modern wives may go to work every morning, but the world still revolved around whether (and who with) half Claribel's clients' husbands fooled around, and whether the other half realized that they—the wives—also fooled around. Contentment must be a kind of death. Imagine getting what you wanted, and having to settle down with it for the rest of your life. Once a man loved you back, and didn't have sexual problems, and didn't cheat on you, and wasn't even married, you daydreamed about him like you daydreamed about your bus pass—you didn't spend your money on a fortune-teller on his account.

And what if happiness had, by some miracle, satisfied anybody? What would Claribel have seen in such a person's cards?

Maybe the tragedy was you had to eat shit before you could appreciate the taste of chocolate. Maybe the tragedy was you never felt so alive as when you sat there with the bucket of shit on the table, and fate put the spoon in your hand.

Heh, heh, heh, heh, cackled her husband in the window, who had long ago formed his own titillating low opinion of her clients. Thank God for the Mayor's wife across the street, to distract him. And for mornings like this one, when Dolora didn't go along in the limousine, but stayed home, keeping him glued to his chair as he tried to pierce the brick walls of her house with his binoculars. *La plus belle mairesse au monde,* he called her, quoting a yellowed newspaper article he carried around in his wallet. How in hell would you know, Claribel snickered now and again with absent-minded malice? You mean to say there ain't a single mayor's wife in the whole world that's better-looking than Dolora Demers? Well ye're an even bigger fool than I thought.

Eh, shaddap, he said.

You shaddap, she said.

Across the street, Dolora, the subject of their bickering and object of his lust, felt stranded in her house where she'd given up even trying to leave an imprint. Victor had bought all the furniture. He'd arranged it himself, for comfort, he said, let's not get artsy-fartsy, we haven't got the room. Yet when the city once considered acquiring a Mayor's mansion, he'd protested adamantly. He would have been too easy to keep track of in there, Dolora supposed. He had to cling to the freedom that came with mobility as he pursued the entries in his day's agenda.

She glanced at her watch. If he had no official luncheon, he'd be holed up in some hotel bedroom by now. How she knew, she couldn't remember: the shock of finding out had subsided too long ago. A guard would be knocking at the door any minute. Time to go, Sir. Victor's guards, for obvious reasons, never addressed him as him Mr. Mayor from outside a hotel bedroom.

And what about Terence? she wondered, feeling abandoned by them both, never begrudging herself the right to feel abandoned by Terence, as well. Wasn't it always he who cancelled their days together at the studio? He who announced, catching her by surprise like a quick fist in the stomach: we'll be closed tomorrow, I'm taking that Minister's portrait to Ottawa? Or that ballerina's or tycoon's to New York or Toronto? He wasn't fooling her. He'd already shipped the portrait. He only wanted to be alone with his new model, whose acres and acres of goose-pimpled, bluish-white meat, sprawled on the podium, he'd made no bones of lusting after.

He must be rolling off her now, onto the hard platform floor, with a sigh and a thump. Another day's light wasted: was it worth it for so little—quality-wise, that is? But then he'd opted for the new model—Dolora knew he had, she was sure of it—only because what he really wanted wasn't on the menu. So he rolled off, and repeated his lie. I've got to go deliver the portrait to Ottawa.

The model never cared enough to bother not believing him.

It had been a long day; and Noel and his crew rammed the service door, and walked out into the first snowflakes as into a swarm of mosquitoes, zipping up their windbreakers.

Eight blocks away, 40 floors up, Blanche, who was black, was staying late to proof-read new leases. Jack observed her, thinking: nice girl, too much a racist to also think: nice tits. Boris smiled as she walked in, unaware that he did, or that he might have conquered the world with a wife like her instead of wasting half his energy on squabbles, and too loyal a husband to even realize he always thought of Lois in Blanche's presence because subconsciously, he compared the two women.

His children would be on their way home by now, just as their mother was getting ready for some evening rehearsal. Why couldn't Lois rehearse in the daytime? Why couldn't she have dinner with her family like everybody else? Never mind. He knew why. Other singers weren't able to rehearse in the daytime, they had to earn a living: that was why. But don't expect Lois to admit it. Don't expect gratitude.

The southshore school bus would be slithering to a stop just about now, and Edith Hobart in her baywindow, watching the children's progress from the corner, her own plus another five or six, including Boris' two, who would by-pass their own homes to converge on her cookies. She was the only full-time housewife on the block. She fed neighbours' children far too many free cookies. And handed out too many free recipes to too many ungrateful mothers, who then only blamed her for their fiascos in the kitchen, whose very contempt was on automatic pilot, who didn't for a minute consider cooking an expertise worth paying for, let alone a talent they might recognize and envy. Would she have had the gall to borrow their only marketable skills? Would she have even thought of asking?

Downtown across the river, snow already greased the streets, already made the porches slippery. Claribel hadn't put down her cocomat runner, and her first clients had to hang onto the bannister with both hands, or if they weren't wearing good coats, slide down the steps on their haunches. They could feel Claribel's husband watching from somewhere inside the house, as they had felt him staring, spying, eavesdropping, creaking in the dark kitchen while they waited their turns in the front parlour. What a creep, they said to one another, hoping he'd overhear them—through the mail slot, maybe, or with his ear glued to the front door.

The bed waits. One day it won't release him. Already, Fabian avoids lying on his back, joining his hands. He's too weak to punch a new hole in his belt. Even his skin is too loose for him. His wife has been predicting his desertion for years. Brilliant and brittle, she has no sense of order, no sense of beauty; or if she had, instead of the prescience she flaunts, he might have never left. According to her, men don't leave alone. Women do, but men fear solitude.

From year to year you forgot about snow, he writes, as women forgot about the pains of childbirth. He senses a smile over his shoulder. He can almost hear the voice. Tst, just like a man to be an expert on the pains of childbirth. This isn't a husky voice: husky voices no longer excite him. This isn't a guttural voice like his wife's. This is a young, a musical voice. The breath smells of apples and celery. The name is Angéline. Something like that.

Fabian has imagined a rainless summer. Late-fall clouds trailing their bloated bellies over the slate-coloured river. And now on the eighth of December, or maybe on the ninth, the sky opening up...

Snow was a blind upside-down, he writes, which the storm pulled up over your windows, while trees and telephone poles and lamp-posts outside grew shorter and shorter like pencils in sharpeners. Boots left little puddles where light trembled. Wives shouted: now don't go trailing slush all over my floors! Men shoved their chairs nearer tables, and buttered their bread with cold red fingers, and fell into their soups. Beyond kitchen doors, angel cakes rose from the lids of garbage cans.

In the morning, the ground glowed. Shovels coughed, children squealed, cars vroomed and skidded.

9

2

Eh, Claribel hisses. At it agin.

Quiet, the old man snaps without turning around. He has Dolora, the Mayor's wife, in his binoculars. He brings her closer, reels her in. She's picking up her milk on the mat from the middle syllable of WELCOME as usual, the cream on the L. She's thinking the milkman must be a Virgo but you can't ask a man if he's a Virgo. A Capricorn or a Sagittarian yes, but not a Virgo. The bodice of her robe gapes as she stoops, and the old man with the binoculars becomes a snowflake on her breast, he mingles with the taste of sleep in her mouth, he's dampness at the back of her neck where hair begins and spreads darkly, he's lost in the scent of all that black hair.

Maybe, Claribel cackles, sallow-skinned and straw-haired behind him: maybe I'll send him an anonymous letter across the street: Dear Mr. Mayor, better watch yer wife, there's a dirty old man spends his days spying on her—

Yeah and I'll send him one about you, Claribel. Dear Mr. Mayor: there's a hag been fortune-telling for years, never bothered her none you passed that law—

You do that so we can go live in some basement on your big pension.

Eh, he shrugs.

Fabian stands up, avoiding the bed. He wants to be out there, with them. He wants someone to rewrite his life. Why can't someone, anyone, have that power—to give him another chance, fresh shirts, plus all the weight he's lost?

Dolora, he sighs.

When he first met her, he asked: is that your real name, Dolora, or is it just your nom de paintbrush? Is that your real name, Fabian, she rejoindered, or is it just your nom de

Casanova? She was already married to the Mayor then, who wasn't Mayor yet. And other men already mumbled: if I should be so lucky as to have a wife like that—

What? he snapped. What would you do?

Last time he saw her she said: ah but you, Fabian, you only write to kill the pain.

She plugs in the percolator. A boy is at the door with two copies of the morning paper, the one, a complimentary subscription.

Your paper, she says to Victor, and walks off with her own.

Victor turns on the bath water. The phone follows him on a long cord. It's part of his image to have only one number, and to live in this modest neighbourhood, although any trespasser who approached close enough to read the brass sign by the door: VICTOR DEMERS, AVOCAT would have to deal with bodyguards.

The radio blares the news on a shelf above the tub. Dolora must imagine it sometimes (or his electric razor, or her hairdryer) falling into the water and sizzling him out of her life: the scene has to be one she'd like to replay.

Across the street, the old wife hisses: you think I don't know ye'd leave me if ye could?

The old man glares, afraid to speak his hatred. Forty years of hatred. Never mind his bad leg. He'd leave if he just knew where she hid her money. Or he could at least daydream about her dying.

Well ye're stuck, she snorts, so used to reading his mind, she's not even aware she's doing it. Not even aware his mind doesn't interest her.

The Mayor's daughters have groped for earplugs on their bedside tables, and squiggled deeper into the covers. If Victor misses them, if he notices they're avoiding him, if he ever wonders why, he has a choice of answers: a) their libertarian friends call him an autocrat; b) everybody knows he keeps a room year-round under an assumed name at some big hotel; c) his gross egotism revolts them, of which this early morning racket is only one example.

He doesn't lower the volume when the phone rings, he only shouts louder: the city has to keep moving! Dolora winces. The caller mumbles something about snow-cleaning crews having been out all night. The radio blares on. We could be in for a hard winter, Mr. Mayor, last time—Victor doesn't need a reminder. Half the outfits went broke. The city bought out the ploughs and blowers cheap. And then blue-collar workers went on strike.

If the storm lasts, we can at least inform journalists the crime rate has gone down, Sir.

As it usually does in a storm. Small mercies.

You might appeal to the public: there's nothing makes the public feel so good as lending a hand.

Ah yes, Victor agrees morosely. And I suppose that should comfort me when my children pretend to sleep until I leave home? When my wife hands me the morning paper and walks away? When the city is besieged by strikes? When even the weather has turned against me?

An unwritten book brims with mystery. Fabian stares at the packet of blank pages. He watches almost as an outsider the letters beginning their journey across. He can barely feel the link there with his consciousness.

At a certain point before the halfway mark, the story will gather momentum. The characters (he's listed the men in one column, the women in another, like guests gathered for a party, which in a sense, they are) will generate energy: they will demand the fatal gift of freedom, and he'll give it to them, he'll let them thrash it out and carry the plot to its conclusion.

Only by the second draft will he take charge again. Pick up the pieces. Draw a master plan, a bird's eye view with some semblance of structure and order.

Between sessions, he shuts his eyes and replays it. Smoother and smoother. Wooing the suspension of his own disbelief.

He remembers the boy across the river climbing up on the window-sill, standing between the glass and the blind, calling his sister. He sees the storm over the insular city as the boy saw it; and then the mother, not the sister, entering behind him. He sees her tugging on his arm and making him lose his balance. She doesn't love him, she never did, he remembers. She raises the blind abruptly, and it clatters against the top of the frame.

And now the father, her husband, calls from the master bedroom, diverting her attention. Poor boring Boris, she grumbles. The boy hears that. Poor boring Boris. But not the rest, not that nothing ever deters him. Not that last night, caught on the bridge for hours, you'd think he would have been too tired to. But no, he's never too tired to. He just slid into bed beside her like a big tremulous squid. weren't you worried about me, Lois? Whereas now, in the sternness of morning: where did you put my new Hermès tie?

She sends the blind flying, darkness irritates her. She finds the tie and holds it up without a word. When she has gone, Boris pulls down the blind again. The boy watches from his bedroom. He recognizes her indifference in the way she has of walking away from his father. The boy realizes: she doesn't love either of us.

Years later, they'll be surfacing in all his fiction under one guise or another. Boris (or Blair or Brent or Brendon), the very sound of his name, a gavel to his rectitude. Lois (or Iris or Chloris or Doris), creative and trapped, her restlessness corroding her affections. Fabian knows her well. If pale, permissive Angéline is a derivative of dark, inhibited Dolora, Lois under all her guises is Fabian's own mother.

He shivers in his two sweaters by the window. The turrets of the hospital rise at the end of the street. He spent a fortnight in a ward up there. Palliative, they called it. A euphemism for: give them what they want for crying out loud, they're dying. He couldn't take so many previews of his own grim end, yet almost stayed because of a nurse who resembled Dolora. He once, years ago, almost had Dolora. But at the last minute she burst into tears, got dressed again, ran out. She left the door open, he heard her rushing down the hotel hall, she didn't even wait for the elevator, she went down the fire exit.

The limousine is at the door. Two guards, not one. She'll be going out, this morning.
    Eh Claribel, asks the old man in the window: where do you figure she goes?

In the house across the street, Victor has brought the phone to the table. He bows, arresting for a moment his bright, beady eyes on the object of his pride, if no longer on that of his affection. But he misses the affection. When they first met, Dolora prattled on radiantly, informing him (as if he cared—but he did, he did!) that there were three great myths: beauty, genius and money; and that all three were traps. She went on to cite her own beauty as an example, as if it were someone else's. It had messed up her life, she said. Men were in awe of her, women envied her, even her own sisters. She stayed home alone Saturday nights while plainer girls had dates. It takes courage to approach a myth, she smiled into Victor's victorious eyes.
    She will never leave him. What kind of a painter would she

be, married to some common little man? Without the perfect dosage only he, Victor, can administer, of humiliation and honour?

He gives, in lieu of greeting, a view of his ungarnished skull. She pushes a mass of curls off her face as if to underline her surplus of what he lacks. She's been dyeing it the past year, and he's often suggested, irritated by the stains in the sink, yet impressed by her frugal dexterity: why don't you go to the hairdresser? She refuses. If I can paint pictures, she says, it stands to reason I can paint hair.

Her friends' husbands have been complaining her artwork is getting too expensive. Growing older and bolder, they've also been finding her beauty less forbidding. Dolora remains elusive. If she won't have it whispered the Mayor's wife dyes her hair, she'll have it rumoured even less the Mayor's wife has lovers.

3

The snow had a miraculous air, that first morning. All night it had come down in large, slow flakes. Now they came faster, finer, harder. A wind was rising and the ground rippled in waves, and from the crests of these waves blew long white hairs.

Guards shuffled their feet at the door. There were more in the bushes because of the strikes. Other times, there were more in the bushes because of threats, scandals, elections, unrest. Victor easily found excuses for guards in the bushes.

What's on the agenda? Dolora asked between the toaster and the poacher. He glanced out. She reminded him she needed four hours at the studio. He would have never bargained for her time at the studio. He had a chronic fear of pushing his luck. In all his years of womanizing he'd never once not once thought of leaving her, whereas she'd threatened him countless times. Of course were he to point this out, she'd only snap he never loved enough to want to leave—not her and not anyone else, love wasn't his bag. He could imagine the tone in which she would say this.

He felt a sadness.

She brought his egg trembling on toast.

He touched her hand.

You want more coffee? the fortune-teller asked, feeling fleeting pity for her old mate's maimed dream of manhood, confined to binoculars in a window.

Suspicious, he shook his head. His eyes remained fixed on the Mayor's house. He wished the door might open. Now when a gust of wind cleared a swath in the storm. Now when he might see her, when he might pick out the mole on her left cheek, the tiny streaks in her make-up. He had a fantasy where she asked him to make her up. All over. He would have been scandalized to know her daughters called him, with amused affection, Mother's Old Voyeur. He would have denounced them vituperously as shameless little whores.

The light outside looked like afternoon, not morning. What would I do without the studio? Dolora wondered. What do women my age do, who have no profession or training, and no small talent to fall back on, to occupy them and give them self-importance? She remembered returning to the studio after the second baby, still smarting from Victor's first infidelities. Terence eyed her gravely. So now we can overcome that fatal facility, he said. She wasn't there for that. She wanted vengeance. But one look at the model on the podium informed her Terence was still up to his old tricks. That if she'd had a chance with him, she'd let it pass, it might have been her last, it wasn't anything constant, anything she could count on, Terence being in his way as variable as Victor.

Sometimes she hates them both.

You're bringing a change of clothes? Victor asks.

You've changed, Terence said, appraising the tightened corners of her mouth, the down-curve of the column of her neck.

She nods. The overnight bag at her feet holds a silk dress, luscious and delicate, moiré shoes, strands of pale, clear stones.

Wear your diamond pin, Victor says. No. As you wish. Why argue with her about small things? Save your breath for when it matters—not that such modest credits ever seem to accrue. Wind rattles the windows. He speaks her name and sees her stiffen. She used to beg, to disengage herself: Victor, please, the children are awake, the car's at the door, the motor running, our guests almost here, the phone ringing, you know I don't like quickies oh my God Victor, no!

Any more coffee?

Workers will be having a second cup, this morning. Later, they'll be nipping over to the Liquor Commission when it opens—this is the kind of weather when they'll do it. A flask keeps you warm on the job. At the wheel of a plough. Aboard snowblowers, trucks and buses. Braving ladders and manholes and slippery stairs and unshovelled sidewalks. Picking up frozen garbage. Transporting short-tempered passengers who'll report you if they so much as smell it on your breath—Victor knows, the reports always filter all the way up to him, in the end.

At eight o'clock on the second day of the storm, which had begun some seventeen hours earlier without fanfare as a snow flurry, and which by dinner-time had been hailed as the first major snowfall of the season—at eight, then, on the second day and first morning of the storm, weather forecasts promised clear skies by noon. Clean streets by evening.

So people shovelled themselves out and went to work as usual.

Noel Masson finds the office open, the boss as usual whistling instructions past a big cigar: when you get there, you'll do the penthouse first and then move all the way down to the lobby. They're having a coupla fancy parties—

In the left column underneath victorious Victor and boring Boris: Noel, a window-washer.

Why, Noel's mother has been asking, wailing in writing if that were possible, and of course as often (not often, thank God) as she's actually spoken to him on the phone: why such a dangerous job? I'd be proud if you risked your life because you were a fireman or a policeman. But to clean windows?

His landlady meanwhile shudders with admiration. Most women do. The younger they are, the more thrilled by any kind of daring, the less concerned with safety. You're like an alpinist, they gush: spending all your days rolling up and down the sheer sides of skyscrapers! You must be scared shitless!

Scared of what? Noel smiles. He loves it, up there. He loves the breezes while pavements sizzle. The broad vistas. The glimpses into the sanctuaries of success. In my line, he likes to point out in his velour voice: the higher the window, the better the view. And the more gorgeous the women who work inside!

But what does a window-washer do for a living in winter? they ask—the women, of course, it's always the women, who ask. I mean, wouldn't water freeze in your buckets at 40 below zero? Wouldn't you die of hypothermia?

Oh we don't go out on scaffoldings between December and March. We'll take on the odd minor exterior job if a client insists. But by and large, we do interiors. Shopping-malls. That sort of thing.

Noel Hasson has never heard an oratorio. He'd be hard put to say what exactly is an oratorio. Were someone to predict: one month from now you'll be singing all the baritone arias from *Japhet's Wife*, he would not only not believe it, he wouldn't know what that person was talking about.

Lois Leduc who will teach him, whom he has never met, whose husband he never deals with because he finds Boris' partner Jack more congenial, Lois is vocalizing this very minute over the roar of her dishwasher while Noel, humming, takes a service elevator to the penthouse of the complex downtown.

From her suburban kitchen, she appraises the storm over the city across the river. Boris' back rises and falls as he shovels the driveway. He's wearing the Hermès tie underneath his parka. One of these days he'll give himself a heart attack, he's the type, tense and fat. Why won't he take a taxi for once? Why does he insist he bought the car so she could at least drive him to the metro station?

Lois daydreams about Boris dying. In her daydream, his partner Jack is her mainstay. Jack organizes the funeral. Holds her elbow in the front pew. Catches her as she faints into the pit of the grave. And then whisks her off to his apartment where he consoles her with unadulterated heat—as opposed to the plaintive and finicky tyranny typical of Boris. Who eats her aura for breakfast. Who puts her aura in the Cuisinart and eats it for breakfast, poor boring voracious Boris. Who comes in now after shovelling and wants more coffee.

You're in no rush, she says.

You have lipstick on your teeth.

She gives a broad, sour smile.

He sighs: can't wait to be rid of me…

I'm going for a major audition, she announces abruptly, like a slap in the face. It takes her courage to do so, she needs the impetus of irritation. Otherwise he'd ask: where? Again? And he'd protest and try to dissuade her. Whereas if she's irritated, she can sidestep sanction, and then accuse him of not having objected until it was too late. Does he consider suburban amateur operetta productions enough for her? Did she once almost star at Covent Garden only to sing at tacky weddings, or for tone-deaf audiences who don't know their Verdi from their Puccini?

He won't dignify such nonsense with a response. He turns his back on her and makes more coffee.

Lois slips into another daydream. In this one, Boris and Jack are picking her up at the studio after the final taping, still in her false eyelashes, her arms brimming with roses. She will have sent herself the roses. She'll say they came without a card, and then drop the card, an ardent, anonymous message, out of her purse at the restaurant. She'll enjoy a restaurant, afterwards. Eating late in public with the two men: the one she hasn't had yet and the one she doesn't want anymore, and with her roses and her false eyelashes, and the elation she only attains when she sings.

I'm bringing Jack to dinner, Boris offers as a peace offering.

The Jack of Hearts?

Who else?

I'll pick you up at the station if you can catch him, she says.

Otherwise I suppose I'll have to walk?

It'll do you good, you're getting fat as a tenor yourself (she's forever comparing tenors to stuffed pigeons).

He sighs, intimating her callousness is the least of her faults, in spite of all of which he loves her. Whereas his own imperfections, few as they are, can alone surmount the wall of her indifference.

But a moment of secret triumph awaits him at the office. Arriving at last, he's caught the Jack of Hearts with his feet on his desk. Oh, if Lois could see him now, the Knave, and never mind Jack! And Hearts, to boot, eh? Why he, Boris, is the fairer of the two. Fairer in more ways than one, he's dared to point out. And she's agreed, she had to, in her clear, treacherous voice: yes dear, fairer and fatter, but fat married men are Kings. You make that sound so dull. Ah but it is, it is. And Jack chimed in, calling him, Boris, august, while Lois insisted the Jack was only a troubadour and a lover. Only a lover, she said. Her words.

All right, seven o'clock at the bar. Jack hangs up. Allo Boris. You're late. Shh—don't tell me. You were stuck on the bridge.

Boris mutters no, he had to shovel the car out of the driveway so Lois could take him to the metro station. Look ar—I take it you're busy tonight—(if he tells her he walked in just as Jack was accepting another invitation, she'll snap: I suppose you dilly-dallied!) Tomorrow then?

Why not?

Boris speculates that in the long run, Jack's mannerisms would be sure to irritate her. He confides she's being difficult, begging for complicity. He draws a blank. He remembers raving about this blue-eyed Italian only a year ago as he strove to cancel her crush of the moment, some amateur basso profondo who sang flat and sold insurance in the daytime. Now he has to put up with hush-hush speculations on the part of Lois' friends and neighbours' wives (he's overheard them, the bitches) that it's got to be Lois Jack is after —why else would he tackle the bridge at rush hour twice a week, after spending all day with Boris at the office?

What did Lois say about the storm? Jack asks, playful. Did she consult her cards?

I didn't get home until after eleven.

Well there have to be some advantages (pronounced: atfantaches) to living in the middle of town.

A secretary is in the doorway, pad in hand. There's always a percentage of unanswered invitations, Sir, but this... She falters. She will record his every twitch, his every curse. Boris thinks of the canapés, thousands of canapés, perishable and expensive. She asks if he came in through the main lobby. Why? The big sculpture's here, Sir. Are they putting it together? It came in one piece. He reads the trace of a smirk on her face. She's going to get the earful she's aiming for. But not yet, he thwarts her a little longer. It couldn't come in one piece, he says. Oh but it did, they dismantled the big doors to let it in, and now nobody knows how to put them back on, and with that wind, there's already snowdrifts piling up against the elevators—Why in hell didn't she tell Jack? Where's Jack! But Jack's disappeared. Vanished. Why don't you ever give him the bad news! You're the boss, she murmurs with insolent meekness. And then delivers the last blow: and the mural for the discothèque, Sir. It hasn't arrived. What! He chokes. He motions to her in mute rage to get out.

When he's alone, he raises his fist toward the ceiling. God damn Lois! he screams, but silently, so the secretaries won't hear him and snicker on the other side of the door. He can thank Lois for this! She was the one suggested the Complex acquire some art. Big pieces, she said, you're the perfect showcase, think of the publicity (her only real concern of course being for her friend Dolora). Oh how she nagged, but then she's always nagging. Always exerting some sort of pressure—Christ, even during sex. Boris, you won't regret it, the Mayor will come to the unveiling, you'll have the press, write-ups, feature stories—

So he gave in against his better judgment. Okay Dolora, so

do me something two meters by five to harmonize with a blue and black décor. Art by the yard? she scoffed, the patronizing twat. And Boris complained to Lois about Dolora's ingratitude. And Lois yelled: you think the Mayor's wife needs a favour from you?

And then the crunch. Six months after commissioning the mural: we've got to know the title of your work, Dolora, we're printing the invitations, our opening's in a few weeks, you haven't forgotten our deadline, have you?

An allegory on love and death, she answered.

He prayed she was kidding.

I'm dead serious—pardon my pun, she said.

He asked, appalled: ar—abstract? hoping it would be abstract as hell.

Oh no Boris, I didn't think you'd like that sort of thing. And she gushed on about the work coming along nicely, about her visits up there after dark to compare her palette to his—

I have no such thing as a palette! he snapped.

But she continued, undeterred: you'd be surprised how even a night sky can vary in colours—

Never mind colours, the news had turned him colour-blind. All he could see was skeletons fornicating on his walls. He almost broke down and wept.

That was six weeks ago.

And the goddam mural still isn't here. Still hasn't been delivered.

4

She refused Victor's arm to negotiate the slippery walk. She sensed eyes in windows, women's on her clothes, men's removing the same. She knew the old one across the street watched her with binoculars, she'd caught him once when a light was turned on behind him and turned off again but not fast enough. Even her guards had the audacity to stare. Victor's adulteries depreciated her. Men respected her less because they pitied her. Why hadn't they, years ago? Why didn't she notice, before she grew too numb to do anything about it?

The car was sleek and cushy. Locked doors. Bullet-proof windows. A second car across the street made a U-turn and followed. Victor snapped open his briefcase almost at the same moment as Dolora tore open her mail. The postman started his route with the Mayor's house, probably paid to do so. The guard beside the driver offered coffee from a thermos. He warned the streets were slippery. The Mayor took the cup as a challenge. Dolora shut the glass partition. She held up a clipping: some of my friends think they do me a favour by sending every criticism printed about you. It's a wonder you have time to read anything else. The car slithered to a stop at a red light. This one's serious. Since when do critics have a sense of humour? The children have been asking— Tell them to come to me. You're never there to explain. They could get up in the morning. They study late. Side with them! It's hard, she sighed. It's sad, Victor said, when a man has to justify himself to his own family. You're the one who should make the overture. If you didn't undermine my influence, Victor shouted, and faltered, the guard up front had started, the driver glanced over his shoulder. Ah, she smiled, bitter: blame me. That's right, like you blame me. You think I have to, she asked dangerously, you think everybody doesn't know? I knew it was you, he said softly. The driver braked. She said, wistful: you used to be such a rebel...And I let you down, he snapped, I didn't by any chance wisen up like everybody else as I grew older, 80% of this city's electorate aren't right about me, only you are right with your suffering silences and accusations behind my back!

They didn't talk the rest of the way. The new courthouse loomed through the snow like an iceberg. Demonstrators had assembled on its doorstep. Placards trembled, tumbled in the wind. Around the corner, in front of City Hall: another delegation, this one in gas masks. Nothing deters them, Victor murmured: teachers will sooner let a kid out of class to picket than to pee. The limousine made a sharp turn into the underground garage. The guard hopped out and held the door open. Victor instructed him: stay with my wife until she goes home or joins me. You (to the driver), after you take her to the studio, come back here and wait.

Dolora wondered: wait for what? What else will Victor be doing later? The chauffeur nodded. If anyone knew the Mayor's secrets, he did. He must regale his wife.

She tugged on Victor's sleeve, detained him as he was about to dash out. Irritation passed in his eyes, followed by a gleam as brief and more surprising. Your driver, she whispered, how come he never says a word, is he mute?

He leaned down to kiss her. He breathed in her ear: had an accident years ago, split his tongue and pierced his palate, instead of suing the city, he came to work for me.

She gasped, repulsed, and yet unexpectedly aroused as if while perusing a perfectly respectable book, she'd stumbled across a dirty picture. Victor's hand touched her thigh: the man I'm sending with you isn't mute, however.

I'll try and give him something to report, she rejoindered. But Victor was already out of earshot, sauntering across the cement floor toward the elevator. He never gave her enough time. It was always quickies or nothing, with Victor. You had to catch him in mid-air, tonight would be too late, someone else would have caught him in mid-air by then.

So Fabian takes his dose and summons Angéline.

At first she's nothing but a shadow in the corner of his eye, which evaporates if he so much as turns to face her. But after half an hour, she has enough substance to walk back and forth across the room. She's abandoned two small children for him, she reminds him. Not to mention their father. Angéline has Dolora's voice but less colour, less flesh.

He leaves the bed. He enters in the left column across Dolora but underneath Victor: Terence.

The apartment adjoined the studio. Dolora had arrived first, and Terence greeted her gladly, the syllables lunging when he spoke her name: Dolora. She folded her arms across her breasts as if (even with her guard here) she needed protection.

Fabian titters, noting that even a half-assed pass causes Dolora to freeze in her mournful unavailability. It will take a vital man to wait. A man in no rush, easily sidetracked.

She feels eyes on her backside as she hangs up her coat. She whirls around and catches the guard staring. Terence is surveying the mural. It's in three parts, like an aria, the central panel in a different key.

Terence flicks on artificial sunshine.

Dolora foresees that her guard too, new to his assignment, will light up like the ceiling when the model takes off her clothes.

The others phone in one by one to say they're stuck at home. They lack Dolora's motivation. They're not all a little in love with Terence. They don't all have shovellers and chauffeurs to help them through a storm. Maybe the model herself will fail to show up at the last minute.

26

But no—that would be too much to hope for. She's here. She flings the door open, panting, dramatic, as if Dolora herself hasn't just come in from the same storm. She's of course aiming her comments at Terence who lives on the premises and hasn't been out.

Terence likes his models massive. He'd chisel giantesses out of marble if he could afford the marble and then could get it up the stairs. He must need a stepladder to mount this one. He must crawl across her pale vastness like a tarantula. She pulls a thermos from her bag. She winks over her shoulder: in my line you gotta warm up from the inside; do I undress now? He says: yes! Enthusiastic. Fascinated by all her activity, drawing life from it. The guard stirs in his corner. Takes off his hat. Lights a cigarette. Makes himself comfortable with his back low on the chair, legs apart.

The model slips off her robe and swings sideways on the platform to recline on one hip and elbow. The guard's eyes, fixed and glazed, yield to lewdness. The model has no choice but to stare back, Terence orders it. Relax, bend your right knee, curl your fingers, look in the corner, there! Dolora intercepts an electricity, maybe a play of power between them, she's not sure, she's never sure to what extent her observations slip into fabrication—it's not everybody that's afraid of looking a man in the face.

Clenching her teeth, she turns her full attention to her canvas.

Victor's beady eyes stare out of it. Only you are civilized, Dolora. The rest of us are all animals.

The guard makes a move. With his coat folded over his arm in front of his crotch, he offers cigarettes around the room.

Dolora watches, mesmerized.

At 6' 5" broad as an armoire, he makes Terence appear over-refined and puny. He approaches the platform last, with deliberate slowness. Holds out the pack in his paddle-sized hand.

The naked model lies all but obliterated between him and the wall. Only her arm emerges, raised toward the proffered cigarette. Only her soft, willing voice. Yeah well I don't mind if I do, yeah well thanks a lot, eh?

Lois was pouring more tea, vocalizing between gulps, inflating the abdomen, expanding the back, pushing down while keeping the jaw wide open, sound oozing from the mask into the room, past the walls, past the wind, over the snowbanks. The neighbour's dog would start to howl in a minute. Babies would fuss. Late sleepers would curse. She might have been a huge hen laying an egg sonorously. She imagined Jack listening on. Being Italian, he'd know enough to be impressed and not embarrassed or amused. Jack would encourage his wife to practise and to sing, wouldn't you, Jack, she'd asked once. That's because he hasn't got one, Boris had snapped.

She wraps her throat in a woollen rainbow. Glosses her lips. Colours her eyelids. Slips on a coat. A cape over the coat. And as an afterthought, phones Edith Hobart who lives across the street: will you take my kids in after school if I get stuck in town? Sure, Edith says. Sure, Lois, why not.

Whoever predicted the weather would clear by noon hasn't read his clouds correctly. The storm has turned into a cauldron of boiling milk. Cars' headlights crawl on the road like pairs of pale moons. An impotent, invisible siren wails as if traffic could untangle to let it through. Lois curses. Then prays. She should have gone on downtown with Boris. She should have parked at the station and taken the metro with him instead of driving all the way back home to dress. But she needed extra time to warm up her voice, and Boris inhibits her, and she would have arrived in a bad mood. For a singer, mood counts.

When she spots the pink stain of a diner's neon sign in the blizzard, she pulls off the road to phone the producer.

I'll be late, you can't imagine what it's like, all of a sudden. He says: go back. She says: not after what I've been through to get this far. He warns sheepishly he may not make it to the metro station to pick her up at the other end. Oh for heaven's sake, she snaps, I'm not a parcel you have to pick up.

5

Traffic had deteriorated. Drivers abandoned their vehicles and walked off with their keys, while others with more nerve, experience or traction honked and shouted and even tried to protest bodily. But no confrontation could last long in such wind, if only because little could be heard above it.

Something collapsed outside. Snow probably sliding off the roof. Blowing off the chimney onto the eaves or gutters.

Claribel snuffed out her cigarette.

We live on my husband's pension, she'll tell her teller tomorrow, when she deposits her pension intact plus a little beside. As if the teller might tell the manager who might rush over to the Minister of Revenue. And her brittle bony hands will flutter on the counter as a proof that two old people don't eat much, you know.

Most of her money she keeps at home. In lamp bases. In the hollows of figurines. Braided inside the braided palm behind the crucifix. On the bottom of powder boxes with the talcum poured back in. Rolled in thimbles. Flattened in cigarette packs. Under cutlery trays. Pinned to underpants. Stuffed

29

inside padded bras. Slipped between the cardboard and the picture, in a frame.

She knows the old fool looks for it the minute she turns her back—searches her jewel box, her purse, her suitcase, her socks, lifts the mattress, rages at her near-empty wallet, thumbs through her books and magazines and hurls them, pounds dents in them with his cane—she knows it's him, who else would it be?

Sometimes to check him before he succeeds she'll leave a bill or two where he can find it, and disappear. Sure enough a case of beer is on its way by the time she comes back, which he'll refuse to share with her as she refuses to share the gin she locks out of his reach. Mine, he'll announce. Bought with *my* money. And she'll titter, knowing how she's fooled him again into thinking he's fooled her. And she'll dance around him like a gnome, asking what else is in his pockets apart from the usual thing he likes to handle so well—money he stole from his wife? And when his gnarled fingers aim for her yellow neck, she'll yap: put them back in, they stink!

Lissten, he cackles. He's got his Bible on his lap, spraying the pages with saliva. The Flood was all on acccounta the womin. I knew I'd seen it someplace, lissten: the sons of God who were descended of Sith, seeing the daughters of man who were descended of Cain, that they were fair, took themselves wives of all that they chose…and they brought forth children… And God seeing that the wickedness of men was great on the earth, and that all thought of their heart was bent on evil at all times, it repented Him that he had made man. There! Bad stock passed on becausa the womin!

And who was Cain to begin with, Claribel snorts: a girl I suppose?

From the likes of what I seen marching in here day in day out, wouldn't surprise me none He did it agin. Bored little

30

adulteresses—

It's you, make them adulteresses with yer dirty mind and yer stinking hands!

And God said to Noah, Behold I will bring the waters of a great flood upon the earth— Ha! The bad stock passed on becausa the womin! Cain fathered nothing but girls, he deserved nothing better!

The phone rings.

Madame Claribel?

It's me.

She reaches for her pad. Speaks in whispers all of a sudden. As if the police were ambushed behind the sofa. Under her very table. Ever been here before? Who referred you? You think you'll make it in this weather? All right and I don't take no husbands. I didn't think you would, the caller murmurs. A smart one. Who's figured out you can't tell a wife she's cheating, and in the same breath do the husband's cards, and tell him the truth.

Be here on time anybody keeps me waiting can go right back where she comes from. She hangs up. Imagine coming over in weather like this, she cries out.

He doesn't respond.

Says it's no big deal—

He plays dead.

Seeing, Claribel continues pointedly, how she lives across the street.

A great shudder goes through him. He struggles out of his chair, his face crimson, and then the colour of oatmeal. He hobbles forward, shaking his cane: you wouldn't bring her in here, he rasps. You wouldn't dare!

Oh no? she cackles. Watch me!

Across town in a windowless studio of the Network Tower, a pudgily pretty blonde has admitted to having a cold, and the producer is shouting she shouldn't be here spreading her germs and wasting his time, and she starts to cry, and blinded by tears, stumbles over to her coat on a stool against the wall.

Okay boys we're folding up. The technicians shuffle in their chairs. Turn off their machines. Click off their luminous panels, and, one by one, the studio floodlights.

It's then, a fraction of a second before the last light disappears, that the vision materializes. Dances in, her fist raised in a sign of triumph, her furs dripping, her teeth flashing, little wet footprints glistening behind her.

The studio has come alive, and seems to be caught in a joyous wind. The pudgily pretty blonde blows her nose, wondering: who's that? The director roars: places everybody! Lois pops a lozenge in her mouth and opens the score on the lectern of the piano. She removes her gloves, hood, cape, coat, scarves. She fluffs out her reddish hair. Clasping her hands, she nods to the pianist and half-shuts her eyes. She drinks the introduction. Raises her cheeks upon the treasure-cove of her mouth into a soulful, melting smile. The blonde is awestruck: am I dreaming, she says, or is that woman singing with a cough drop in her mouth?

Dolora had transposed in a dark corner of the canvas the carnal pallor of the model. She busied herself about it, ignoring Terence who stood behind her, enormously amused. I seem to recognize your famous husband's beady little eyes, he whispered. And he lingered and watched as she elongated the ovals and drew them closer together. Lowered the lids. Emphasized an air of self-conscious sexuality, of hardened experience, which in Victor was more dynamic yet more subtle, more concealed. And then altered the eyebrows, because it was in the eyebrows as well as in the degree of openness of the eyes, that expression resided.

Terence burst out laughing giddily. It was obvious from the

portrait that Dolora was jealous of his model.

An idea leapt in him.

Come on let's have coffee, he says.

The guard snaps to attention. Now wait a minit. The Mayor gave strict orders—

Terence waves him off. The door clicks shut behind him and Dolora.

Silence hangs in the studio like the smoke of the two cigarettes.

The model swivels on the podium to put her feet on the floor. Her knees don't quite touch. Her knowing eyes never leave the guard's face. She registers his reaction, a small flash of almost-pain. She's done this a thousand times, she might be checking an electric outlet.

They got nerve, she says.

The guard defends Dolora. She's not like that, she's a lady.

Ladies turn you on?

He looks congested. No.

She slips on the robe but doesn't tie it. Would you like a spot of tea? she offers, parodying a lady's gentility. She yawns and stretches, inches from him, and then sits down again. The robe falls like draperies on either side of her hips. He tries not to look down the inch or so of space between her knees. She refills the thermos cup for him.

Thanks. Too soon. He has touched her. She has a tiny smile, a flicker of triumph. She hands him the cup and drinks direct from the thermos. She dribbles, and seems to enjoy that, to revel in it. His eyes follow the droplets down her chin and chest and belly. He gulps. He chokes on the straight rye but drains the cup.

In the adjoining apartment, windows resembled paintings of a blizzard, and gave off a pale and otherworldly light. Sipping coffee under a circle of warmer light, Dolora felt enclosed, islanded—shipwrecked. The man who sat across the table from her had little in common with the Terence of her daydreams. She'd been at ease with him as long as they stayed in the studio. But push that other door, and he became edgy. He made her nervous. She might have picked him up in a dark alley. He might be the sort of stranger your mother told you not to talk to. Even his voice sounded different. Even his silences were troubling, compelling her to fill every pause with chatter as if it were a dog she had to throw meat to.

She had chosen to be a dreamer. She saw that now, with a kind of bemused horror. She had settled for the innocuousness of daydreams over the dangers and ravages of experience. She had enjoyed daydreams for their own sake. She had allowed them to spoil reality for her, to disperse the energy that hope requires in order to be fulfilled

But Terence was here. The real Terence. Fifteen years too late. For the first time in a long time, his desire focused on her. His eyes clung to her over the rim of his cup. He was a big black hole in space just waiting to draw her into its vortex. She bolted upright. Her chair toppled backwards.

He had grabbed her from behind, clutching her buttocks. She froze, humiliated.

He looked puzzled. Sour.

They stared at each other.

He stood up, gathered his cup and went to rattle it in the sink. She went to stand beside him, she longed to touch him, but didn't dare. He turned the water on full blast. He pummelled the garbage can to dispose of the old coffee filter. He started the rumble and swish of the dishwasher. Then without looking at her, he snapped: what are you waiting for? Let's go.

He opened the door to the studio. He rammed it shut.

For a moment, she didn't understand. Then she did, and laughed and laughed until she cried. And then she slipped gears. She wasn't laughing to tears, she was weeping, she was regretting and lamenting all the loneliness, all the lovelessness of her life.

If he would only hold me now, she thought. If he would only say don't cry, don't cry, and hold me!

But he just stood there, embarrassed and distant and puzzled, while snow pelted the windows with a granular sound.

6

At the Panorama Restaurant, Jack as usual had ordered what turned out to be the better meal. Afterwards, on a full stomach, he daydreamed of quick routes to suburbia while Boris with a pained expression and a half-untouched plate complained new tenants wanted to see him at four—in this weather.

Jack mused: wannerful, wannerful.

Boris fidgeted with the utensils: they're asking for two floors, we'll have to move people around, you're good at that.

Small-time diplomacy, Jack agreed, realizing Lois was going to be alone tonight. Her breasts in an angora sweater. Her voice like a bell forgotten but for an occasional tug from the wind. He'd like to ring her an Angelus. He'd like to ring her a wedding and a christening and a goddam Easter morning. He'd like to ring her a papal visit for crying out loud.

You'll have to check on those windows, Boris was saying. Jack sighed, easing out of his chair. He would have loved a second cup of coffee.

He found Noel in the lobby. A long, muscular figure topped by a long, square face. Fluent English. No flask in the pocket, no cigarettes. Had any lunch, he asked? The storm assailed the plate glass like a swarm of white locusts. Noel smiled: breakfast at seven, lunch at twelve, I don't work on my ass, me.

Delivery trucks hadn't made it into the city after the weekend. The cafeteria had run out of milk. Jack squeezed into a telephone booth to cancel the evening's engagement. He emerged tittering. Expressions such as Something has come up, and You're pulling my leg, confirmed his belief in the subconscious hypocrisy of the English language. He whispered almost audibly: Lois. A sound of flesh pumping into viscous flesh. Lois.

In Greek, someone had once told Lois (but she forgot who) they called it a crown (*corona*) this final sustained high note, the sound-equivalent of a dancer's pirouette or of a skater's spin. It always drew applause.

Afterwards, trading the staid cold of the marble halls for the live cold of the storm outside, she left the Network Tower with a laughing, lifting feeling of power.

Use the pay phone here, Fabian whispers, propelling Angéline into a slightly seedy hallway: who cares who overhears you? A redhead in a green dress emerges from a door across the landing. Full green thighs. Angéline disappears so Fabian can stare at her. The mailman clanks the boxes down below. I thought you'd never get here, the redhead shouts down! You're lucky I got this far, the postman shouts up! Fabian reflects it's a bad habit to want mail, it's a dependency he should have outgrown, he should be relieved nothing comes anymore from the wife he's left, the mistresses who didn't last, the children who don't know where he lives.

The redhead shrinks against the bannister to let him pass. What does she think he has: a social disease? Phone from here, he urges Angéline. He's tired, he must retrieve his bed. He leaves the door ajar. Another door squeaks along the phone wall. A man emerges, youthful at a distance but less so in close-up, who soon returns with his letters, slamming the door behind him, and causing the pay phone on the wall to give a faint ring. Fabian listens. He can't hear the fall of Angéline's coin let alone her conversation. He calls her. She stands on the threshold. My son is sick, she says, I have to go home. He doesn't reproach her: you still call it home. He asks: what's wrong? She says: they don't know. Or maybe: pneumonia. Or maybe: appendicitis. He'll have to decide what it is that she answers.

When the phone rings, the four of them start. Dolora thinks: it's Victor, and notices the model's thighs quivering, and imagines that Victor would enjoy this. Terence asks without meeting her eye: you know a Jack Niccolini? She shakes her head. Are you sure you want to speak to Mrs. Demers? Yes, Jack insists at the other end, I'm Boris Leduc's associate, it's about a mural she was to have delivered... Ah yes we have a mural here, we'll be taking it across the plaza as soon as the weather clears.

Victor phones within minutes. He's frantic. He's sending a snowmobile for her, there'll be no party tonight, he doesn't know when he'll be home, or if he'll be home at all.

With a pin she scratches her name in the dry paint in a corner of the central panel. She must tell Lois the work is finished and a success, and tell her to tell Boris not to worry, it'll be there on time oh and please thank him. She must remember to tell Lois to thank him.

But Lois isn't home. Lois is at a pay phone asking in a disguised accent if she may speak to Mr. Jack. That's how they call him at the office, while with Boris, it's *Mossieu* Leduc, mockingly.

She doesn't have to identify herself. Jack claims that being the caller is enough of a concession. (The truth is Jack believes inquisitive operators hinder hanky-panky.) Lois is told Mr. Jack has gone home for the day.

On an impulse, she takes the metro to Peel street instead of to the south shore line. She braves the storm again at the exit. She laughs at the hem of her cape which brushes the snow behind her, at her boots which sink in above the rim at every step. She hardly feels the cold on her face between the hood pulled down to her eyes and the scarf pulled up above her nose. She tackles the hill almost effortlessly, telling herself she's a fool, yet not considering for a moment that Jack might not be home. Or home but not happy to see her. Or home but not alone. You, you at last, Lois, he will whisper hoarsely!

She has the key to his apartment. He gave it to her last summer before going to Italy—to her and not to Boris, knowing how much more she would appreciate his trust (pronouncing it thrust, on purpose). Don't make any special trips, Lois. Just—if you happen to pass by, water my plants. Which she did. Not only watered but fertilized. And dusted. Not only the plants but the furniture. The window-sills. And vacuumed the floors, leaving in his fridge "a feastlet," as she called it, for his return. He declared afterwards she'd waved a magic wand over his whole apartment. You're the one with the wand, she protested. I felt your touch, he continued, everywhere. And they giggled, the two of them, while Boris clucked humourlessly.

She'll say: oh Jack I got the lead, you've always encouraged me, let's celebrate together before I go home and Boris gives me hell! That should do it. He'll embrace her somewhat longer than necessary because of her trek through the storm. And elated and shivering, she'll respond also longer. And they'll ignite. She's planned it a thousand times, imagined a variety of contexts and excuses, all of them leading to the same

38

gloriously unavoidable outcome. Ignition.

She rings the door downstairs as a matter of courtesy and precaution. She doesn't wait for the buzzer, she has the key. She's ready for anything and eager for it. Jack in a loin cloth dripping his way from the tub to the door. Or barring the entrance because a girl is in the tub with him or no, in bed, in which case he won't drip, or anyway not all over. Lois' mouth goes dry.

Upstairs, she considers ringing again. She opts for giving him time. She stares at the brass number on the dark varnished wood, and at the peephole that looks out, not in, and at the handle he will turn any second. She asks herself: what am I doing here? Who am I? And the moment tears from the rest of her life like a page from a book. She finally forces herself to push the button. She hears the chime inside. She listens for movement. She counts to 30. Rings again. Counts again. Then slowly tries the lock.

She pauses in the foyer. She listens for steps or voices or music or running water—what if he's in the can? How would he like her arriving just when his laxative was working? What if he's ill and fate has brought her in the nick of time? She dwells on that one a little. Or maybe just asleep, snoring under a comforter. The bedroom door is shut. He'd emerge from a dream, unguarded, believing her to be part of the dream, she'd fall in with him in slow motion, dreaming his dream, mingling her leaves with his, encountering his hard live branches.

She calls: Anybody home?

What's your name, the Mayor asks? Snow melts from the man's hair onto his shoulders: Campo. Ah yes, Campo, we spent a fortune on snow removal last year, Mr. Campo. The man fidgets with his wet gloves: I don't recall getting rich, he says. We signed a contract, Mr. Campo, nobody twisted your arm; and now before winter begins— Begins, Campo shouts!

39

They're calling this the storm of the century!

A motley procession paces in front of City Hall. Placards collapse over smudged slogans. The ghosts of fists rise and freeze. Curses die of cold between teeth. A guard watches from a window, thinking: I owe them my job, the poor buggers.

We were working overtime all last night, Campo sighs. You'll be working tonight, Victor threatens. There's so much snow out there, even the ploughs are getting stuck, we can't clean the streets until the traffic clears and the traffic can't clear until we clean the streets. The Mayor's eyes gleam: I do the impossible all the time, Mr. Campo, tell me, is it snow we're talking about, or money?

The phone rings. He picks it up. In a deadlock, he doesn't aim at convincing, so much as at appearing impregnable. Objections are tolerated, albeit futile. A secretary touches Campo's elbow: why don't you make yourself comfortable, this could take time...long distance... Campo stares at her: how does she know, she didn't answer it—some little tart, more likely. The Mayor swivels away from the desk towards the window. The guard glances at him thinking: the nerva those whores phoning in the middle of a meeting, his own wife wouldn't dare. Your Worship, announces a deep voice on the line, I've got the latest weather report. The Mayor winks over his shoulder at Campo who finds him looking tired, and feels his anger falling like the goddam snow outside. So what if the Mayor has a little tart here and there, a man needs heat in this weather. Someone pushes a scotch in front of him. A platter of sandwiches. Would he prefer coffee? It's going to be snowing another twelve hours, says the voice on the phone: there's three more disturbances lining up in that storm track. The Mayor nods, looking very grave. Campo, observing him, wonders if the tart is telling him she's got a herpes. Or worse.

The binoculars have slipped off his lap with a dull thud and Claribel is hopping beside him, pointing at the curtains:

Him across the street! Her husband! The witch hunter! He's just declared a state of emergency!

Eh, he says. Ye woke me up with all yer shouting.

Just like you to wait for her all day, and then go fall asleep a minit before she comes home!

Ye're lying. He turns on her: and I can't believe ye git a client on a day not fit for a dog, and ye manage to go smell like a distillery before she arrives. One whiff at you, she'll change her mind. Who needs an old witch who's a boozer to boot.

Ye were dead to the world and she came home, Claribel gloats. I saw her!

That's a lie, he says: ye're so drunk ye're seeing things.

But fences had disappeared. Hedges. Hydrants. Basement windows. Porch steps. And as soon as ploughs cleared the snow, more fell in, pedestrians glancing back only to see the channels closing behind them, headlights crawling in the blizzard like phosphorescent fish.

7

Lois suspended her damp coat and cape over the tub to dry, leaving her boots under the radiator on a boot tray she'd given Jack last Christmas. You need a boot tray in this country, Jack. A tray for *boots*? he'd exclaimed, incredulous, staring at the large package. Silver? Oh no, no, no! And now she dialled the number of the office again, and Boris shouted: where have you been! And she snapped: must you pretend to forget I had an audition?

How did it go?

What do you think?

His predictable reaction of stunned disapproval justified her pursuit of a consolation. Big clients were in the conference-room now, he said morosely, and would likely be there for hours. Ah, and her friend the Mayor's wife hadn't delivered the mural: I don't suppose you could speed her up, nag her as you nag me?

Lois took her cue: since when do I do your dirty work, where's Jack anyway, why doesn't he do it?

Jack's gone home.

She managed to hang up, knocking the phone off the table in her haste. Jack would be here any minute. She could hear steps, probably his, coming down the hall now.

She decided she would greet him without a word. The scenario changed once he arrived to find her, and not vice-versa. She would stand facing the door with her breasts heaving. He would know in a flash why she was here, and pause, paralyzed with desire, maybe stalled under the siege of some misplaced loyalty. In which case she would cross the room toward him *molto lento. Pianissimo. Con passionate retinuto.*

But after half an hour, her trepidation wilted. The apartment was overheated. Her eyes were closing. She must lie down. When Jack arrived she'd explain how walking in all that wind had made her sleepy, and he'd sit on the bed beside her and— Or she'd pretend to sleep and let him play the Prince to her Sleeping Beauty. She enjoyed Sleeping Beauty fantasies, when sleepy.

She felt in her head small sudden pockets of darkness. She peeled off her clothes sloppily. The bed felt cool.

Her eyes snapped open.

Jack's scent was on the pillow.

All of a sudden she craved the proof that he wanted her. The undeterrable stolidity of his face. The rush of his breath in her ear. His weight, crushing her pelvis. *Marriage is the union of meat.* Who was it that wrote that? How true it would be if she were married to Jack! And she clutched the pillow between her thighs. And she jabbed the silence, over and over, with the sound of his name.

Lois, Jack whispers. Lois. To goad himself on, and then as a sustaining thought when the crowd traps him and the corner of a briefcase threatens to crush his knee cap. There are already too many people down in the metro stations. He hasn't made it into the first train, doesn't into the second, and is about to miss a third when he remembers Boris calling him a doormat and a pushover. He rams through a family, dispersing it, and jumps aboard as the whistle screams. He rides with his coat tail caught in the door. He transfers to the south shore line where the crowd carries him like a current.

He never enjoys the ride under the river. He can't remain unaware of that huge rush of water, icy and polluted. He can't not imagine a fissure, the tunnel caving in, the panic of the doomed passengers, the screams, aaaghhh—

When the track runs uphill, he breathes easier. The train rocks on its rubber wheels. Lois, he keeps whispering like a mantra. Lois. How will I ever get from the station to Lois? It's too cold to walk, there's bound to be a shortage of taxis; and buses, if any, will be overcrowded and slow. And then of course, she'll have the children. Never mind, he'll talk to them, intelligent and sincere: your father's stuck in town, he asked me to look after you. She'll send them to bed early, you need more sleep when it's cold. And afterwards—Madonna— her eyes shining in the glow from the fireplace. A log throwing off sparks. She, giving a melodious gurgle. He, kissing her on her gurgle. Swallowing the voice warm from the throat, finding the throat wide open, all her doors open, front door, back door, side door, windows, even the doggie door and the mail slot if she has one. He titters. People stare. He checks himself.

The crowd hoists him upwards. The blizzard attacks him at the exit. His coat flares like a flame, his hat is a kite without a string: my hat! my hat! he cries, trying to keep his coat down, and meanwhile his eyeballs freezing in their sockets. Madonna forget the hat, just please make somebody give me a lift!

What are you doing here, a woman shouts? Me? You, she points at him: isn't this your hat? But she falters—can't remember his name. Niccolini! he exults; and clasps the hand that clasps the hat. She turns toward a shadow in the whirling white dusk: dear, remember—Jack Niccolini, Jack shouts, amazed she can see and hear, let alone recognize and remember. But where from, where from, he wonders; and she volunteers as if reading his mind: the Leducs' costume party! My Gad, such memory! He almost embraces her, listening for a jingle of car keys. Who'd ever forget the Jack of Hearts, she shouts above the wind? But before she starts recounting how Lois had to force him to wear those red leotards, he interrupts her to concentrate on the husband. He knows most husbands enjoy the spectacle of their flirting wives ignored. I'm going to the Leducs now, he says pointedly, I hope to Gad the buses are running. The response is reluctant, albeit dictated by the fact an extra man might come in handy, should the car need a push. Well ar—hop in with us.

The wife motions to him to sit up front with her. Another starved suburban housewife. Sach opportunities. Jack wisely gets in the back. He makes a point of stretching with pleasure; and the motor hums, and the wheels skid, and the windshield frosts over. He wipes the frost off the windows with his gloves.

The husband thanks him. Jack smiles at the wife who smiles back through the rear-view mirror. I'll never forget this as long as I live, he gushes. Then as he peers outside, it occurs to him he may not live that long. Every ten minutes or so, he hops out to clear excess snow from the rear windshield. Passengers of other vehicles are doing the same. The road is strung in both directions with a double strand of headlights growing dimmer and dimmer.

By the time they reach the traffic circle, the three have lapsed into tense silence. The husband has switched on the radio to reports of the weather: all accesses impracticable. Side streets, main thoroughfares blocked solid, highways closed in a radius of 40 miles, citizens urged to stay where they are as the Mayor declares a state of emergency...Now on the international scene— Who cares about the international scene, Jack interrupts, to prove that although a foreigner, he identifies with the locals. The wife nods, the husband tunes in to another station: several major accidents... Airport shut down... Now official that buses and trains will not be moving in or out of the city...

I always imagine trains ramming through no matter what, the wife says in a small scared voice.

But Jack exults in the revenge of nature. Of course, he makes no mention of Lois. Or of the fact that he counts on the weather to keep Boris away.

This is one helluva night, the husband muses. I mean you must be one helluva friend to be coming over to dinner on a night like this...

The room had burst into light without warning. The old man was shouting: I told ye never to do that!

Nobody kin see you through all that snow, Claribel shouted back!

I don't care, I told ye never, never—

45

I'm looking for my appointment book!

Eh, you're always looking for your appointment book!

I left it here! she insisted, knowing he liked nothing better than to finish her drink the minute she turned her back, to eat off her plate while she answered the phone, to hide her newspaper, her glasses, her appointment book, anything she needed or valued, besides, of course, stealing her money as often as she let him.

Their eyes met.

Can she possibly hate me as much as I hate her, he wonders? And his horror feels fresh, newborn, he pauses to be aware of it as if for the first time.

She disappears into the kitchen.

The agenda she's looking for is under the Bible on his lap. He's already ascertained her next client won't be the Mayor's wife. But he wants one more look before he calls out: I've found it! Before she asks: where? Before he shouts: under the table! Before she snaps: eh, I wonder how it got there! Before he cackles: it walked, eh, heh, heh, heh!

He counts the fortunes she told last week. She made a killing, poor as she claims to be. Some people make fortunes, some only tell them, poor me, she says. He memorizes a number. A snooty little whore's, who came on Friday at seven, a nine-three-three exchange from the west end of town. Mousy hair. Small tits. He's going to phone her. He's going to whisper to her words she'll never learn in no book... Nine-three-three, he cackles softly. Nine-three-three...Eh, I found it! he calls out. Eh Claribel, I found it, yer appointment book!

There are no porches to the bungalows on this side of the street, only a roof over the door, held up by columns, and snow already halfway up them; and Jack sinks in to the knees at every step on his way to the back of the house, knocking at a patio door, a kitchen door, a garage door, remembering how he imagined all her doors earlier; but in his daydream, they were a lot more hospitable.

He laughs grimly. He tries the windows, he peeks inside, hoping to discover some light somewhere, maybe the doorbell's not working.

Every step allows more snow into his pant legs. If he dies of cold behind the house, it will be days before they find him. He turns back. The wind catches him as he rounds a corner and hurls him against a wall. He thinks of breaking a window. He can't, he might cut himself and bleed to death with the storm inside the house, and no doctor. Madonna, I'll never have a dirty thought about that woman again—where is she anyway? Is it possible her garden was still abloom with roses, just a few weeks ago? He clambers over a buried hedge toward the next door neighbours. He hopes they aren't the ones who own the dog that starts to howl everytime Lois starts to sing.

He leans on the bell.

A young girl opens the door without unhooking the chain. I'm locked out! he pleads over the wind, and a sheet of snow blows in sideways through the opening. I came to see the Leducs but nobody's home—you know the Leducs? She positions herself across the gap: I'm just the babysitter! The snow continues to blow in over her head. Jack says: Mr. Leduc is stuck downtown, he sent me here to look after his family but either nobody's home or they're not answering the door! And he enumerates every possible, even implausible, disaster, sprinkling his conjectures with slang and clichés. He has a foreigner's taste for slang and clichés, the one because it normalizes him, the others because they retain for him the impact of fresh images. Where are those kids now, he asks the girl? How should I know, she rejoins nervously? He tries to laugh: I musta had a hole in my head when I decided to come all this way! But he only manages to look more desperate and more insane. He catches sight of his reflection in the glass of the

47

side-light. His face dissolves, he's sobbing under the frozen skin of his face. The girl gesticulates: the schoolbus left a bunch of kids across the street over there! And as he turns to look where, she slams the door shut, he can hear the inner door slamming as well, the locks turning, the bolts sliding. He drags himself to a window, brushes enough snow off it to peek inside. She stares back, tracked. Two small children hug her knees, shrieking mutely on the other side of the glass.

It's always when you don't want them that you get them, Lois reflects; and fearful Jack may show up now, she makes the bed, makes coffee. Only afterwards does she dial her neighbour's number to verify her children got there safely. The line is busy. A babysitter across the street is on the phone, warning Edith Hobart a man just came by looking for the Leduc children, some nut with a foreign accent, I had to tell him where they were Mrs. Hobart. Edith hangs up, 5′ 10″, 140 pounds. She fetches her husband's hunting-rifle from a cupboard in the den while the foreigner struggles across the street. When she hears him on the porch, she lifts the flap of the mail-slot and yells: what do you want? Jack pushes in his credit cards. What the hell, she says. You got to know who I am, I work with Boris Leduc, I'm his associate! She recognizes a mugshot on an ID card: hey weren't you at that Halloween party? Yes he cries gratefully, yes: the Jack of Hearts! She hides the rifle at the back of the coat closet and unlatches the door. Jack stumbles in. She gasps: how long have you been out there? Too long, he says, fighting an urge to weep again. She brushes the snow off him with a broom, and takes his coat, and offers a warm robe and mouton slippers, which he accepts, awash in gratitude. The phone rings. She doesn't run to answer it, but recedes on very long legs like an undertow swishing off a beach, majestic. How didn't I notice her at that party, Jack marvels? Lois of course monopolized his attention, dressed as *Les fleurs du mal* with a bunch of anthuriums on her head, whereas this one, if her present outfit can serve as an indicator, must have been on the drab side of happy-go-lucky. Your kids are fine, fine, he overhears her trumpeting on the phone from the kitchen, the voice a good match for the rest of her person. Listen, there's somebody half-frozen to death got here God only knows how, all the way from downtown looking for you, Eyetalian chap— what's your name, she shouts? Niccolini! Edith relays the message to Lois who sits on the edge of Jack's bed, and hovers between laughing and crying. Let me talk to him. She hears the blare of Edith's summons. Then Jack. Grave. Caressing. I thought you couldn't make it tonight, she says. He can't admit in front of Edith that Boris' absence makes all the difference: discretion checks him, plus of course self-interest. He says: Boris will be late, I was worried about you and the children. He realizes it doesn't occur to Lois to be jealous of Edith. He thanks his lucky star. He adds: I felt you shouldn't be left alone out here, Boris didn't actually ask but— He thinks you went home, Lois interrupts. I nearly did. What a shame. What do you mean? Guess where I am? Oh no. He collapses onto one of the Hobarts' vinyl kitchen chairs. I have a key, remember? *Porca miseria.* After hoping for months she'd use that key. After feeling unfaithful, not to mention nervous, everytime he settled on a substitute: unable to undress a girl without first checking out Lois' whereabouts— You never get them when you want them, do you, Jack. Speak for yourself, he says staunchly, I always get what I want in the end. And he hangs up with a look of longing toward Edith, which he is chivalrous and devious enough to disguise as an amorous sigh into Lois' ear. His hand still on the receiver, he asks himself: could I be so lucky as to have Edith here, and then go home and find Lois still there? But could my heart take such good luck, for starters—let alone could I take all the complications?

He accepts a drink. Edith propels him to a deep, drab sofa

in front of a fireplace. She drops into an armchair at an angle from him. Her knit dress molds the tops of her long, lean thighs, revealing their undersides as she crosses her legs. So what's between you and Lois, she asks? What's your name again, he rejoinders? She smiles: Edith. He raises his glass: to Edith. She holds his eye: to the Jack of Hearts.

He bursts out laughing. He feels his lips vibrating on the rim of his glass. He smells the casserole in the oven. He hears the children in the basement. He feels safe and cosy and almost unbearably lucky.

8

From the hall at the core of the building you couldn't hear the storm. But the minute someone opened a door, the wind rumbled in the distance against all that glass, like a huge rolling-pin.

A number of people who'd tried to leave too late, or lived too far and knew from the first that they could never make it, milled about the office, chattering excitedly about buried metro exits, thousands of cars abandoned on main arteries, drifts as big as houses on the plaza downstairs right outside the main entrance—

Noel waved his time-sheet.

I can't sign anything, I'm at the switchboard, a young woman said. or: I only do files. or: I'm in accounts receivable. And their innumerable tiny feet rushed past his boots like minnows swimming by a couple of beached whales. Imagine a coffee shop without coffee, they babbled. Cafeterias picked clean…line-ups a mile long…buy candy while you can… Mr.

Jack would have got us food before it came to this, but him in there— And they glared at the boardroom door, and then noticed Noel and faltered.

I'm no spy, he mumbled.

A door clicked open at the end of the hall.

A girl emerged, dark as the leather chair he was sitting on, and as softly lustrous. He watched her approach between the pale partitions. Moon-like eyes, the whites so white, they formed crescents around the irises. Purple lips. He wondered what it would be like— He flushed. She had halted in front of him. His heart pounded. She asked: are you waiting for someone? He rose and stuttered: I ar—got to get this time-sheet signed—

She took it and rushed away.

And now he could watch her swaying from the rear. He could admire her high, round ass.

When she returned, she asked if he wanted coffee; and he forgot he only wanted to go home, and said yes, and followed her to the coffee machine. He realized he'd never smell fresh coffee again without remembering her dark presence beside him.

She motioned him to a bench. She handed him a cup, her fingers brown on the white styrofoam. When her head strained for a sip on her long neck, he thought of a black swan eating white bread. He found himself recalling phrases from the Bible. Black but beautiful. Full of grace. They sipped in unison, his right arm rose as a reflection of hers, he felt extraordinarily aware, he had an eerie feeling there was no need for words between him and this girl, as if they were spirits, or members of a tribe that hadn't developed speech. He felt a loss of control. He tried to normalize the moment, he summoned to his rescue his prejudices, his superstitions, he stood them on the carpet before him. They had ceased to exist. He tried small talk. She only rounded her eyes: pardon? The pupil moist and ripe. The rims enormously white. She smiled, her teeth so perfect, he wondered: are they real? And then she remembered to ask, alarmed: was it just you, waiting, or your whole crew? And he answered: just me, and flushed, thinking that to any other girl he might have answered: just you and me, Babe. But to her, he only, humbly answered: no, just me.

Someone opened a door. He saw the wall of windows. He heard not only the rumble of the wind, but inexhaustible millions and millions of tiny pellets on the surface of the glass, wave after wave of them, pulsing like his blood, like the very beating of his heart.

Pain will have to get closer, harder. He doesn't even notice it at first other than indirectly, not because he's afraid (he has morphine until tomorrow) but because he forgets to feel grateful for feeling comfortable.

At the beginning of his illness, he thought he had a copyright on pain. He felt it set him apart, made him special. Before that and as far back as he can remember, he was always on the lookout for beauty because it reassured him, because it proved all hope wasn't lost for the world, after all. Now he looks for pain because it makes him feel normal. He'll notice cripples. Kids who look like addicts. Children who look abused. Wives who look battered. Men who look trapped. Pregnant women who have that unavoidable pain ahead of them. He'll imagine migraines and backaches, toothaches and arthritis. He'll branch out into grief and violence, alcoholism and abandonment, despair, depression, debt, divorce. Anybody free from pain out there? Anybody who doesn't hurt one way or another?

He considers himself fortunate because nothing more can happen to him: there just isn't time. His children are grown, they can hardly pre-decease him and even if they did, it wouldn't be for long. Plus his heart's already broken, not to mention that hepatitis, and now this—

His face is clammy. He shuts his eyes. Stranded commuters invade the metro levels like armies of red ants, devouring everything.

He wipes his face. The cars are abandoned bumper to bumper on the street below. He visualizes a string of head-lights on the long sweep of *Côte des Neiges,* Snow Hill. Names recover such freshness in translation. Like prim de Maison-neuve, taking on rakish airs as Casanova Boulevard.

He emits a shallow chuckle, more like a moan.

He fumbles for the syringe. He tries to steady his hand.

The needle finds its target. He winces. He sees in red letters the names of the women he's loved. He sees them enjoying his pain, having wished it on him. He's not afraid of death, only of pain. He gasps. He claws the air. He turns on the radio for company. An immense well-being floods him. A bus was found stalled in a residential neighbourhood with all its passengers dead of carbon monoxide. What a lovely death. His prayer will be answered as few ever are, or can even be called prayers: a quiet, whole, unbloodied death, the ravage internal, invisible—the ultimate politeness.

His only regret is that Angéline has gone. After he invented her so she'd be with him now, she assumed a life of her own, they all do, the ungrateful wretches, she's on her way home, I have to go home, she says. She's arrived. She re-enters her old house as a stranger: it feels familiar and yet different; and the mixture makes her lightheaded, as if she were dreaming. Only the odours are still absolutely the same, and assault her with a rush of memories, plucking that cord in the brain that stores and replays the past. Her boots go stand in their old corner. She grips the bannister as she used to, pulling herself up a little with each step, recognizing now this small creak, now that, under certain parts of the design in the carpet. For a moment she feels she's never left.

She hears her husband at the door. She hears heavy feet on the stairs.

She's lost the habit of his looks, of his voice. But not of the smell of alcohol that walks into the room with him.

When Victor caroused, Dolora was abandoned. But when he worked, when he spent the night at City Hall, her solitude assumed a dimension. A dignity.

She glanced outside at the lumps in the snow. Did birds and squirrels ever freeze to death? Or pets locked out? Or kids arriving at the door to find it buried, glued shut by ice, the parents stuck downtown, neighbours not at home, every door on the block frozen shut and buried?

The phone rang: I got you an appointment—no of course not, I didn't give her your name, what do you think I am, crazy?

She switched on more light, but the house remained dim. Lamps didn't conquer its shadows. Snow melted from her hair down the back of her dress.

I must call Lois, she thought. I must not forget to call Lois.

But Lois had gone, leaving her panties as a calling card under Jack's pillow. She'd stepped outside, where the storm hurled itself at her in waves, like a surf. And with surprise, no longer propped up by the prospect of meeting Jack, she sensed danger.

She hesitated. She considered not even attempting the descent to the office. The alternative—the overheated apartment upstairs—depressed her.

Skyscrapers lined the hill like phosphorescent giants. ploughs growled on the edge of traffic, while policemen on snowmobiles and skis forced passengers out of their cars: it's no use staying in there, Madam, Sir, if this weather lasts another hour we'll never be able to get you out. Only pedestrians were still able to move, taking their journeys one phase at the time, from one building's lobby to the next.

She joined their throng. She felt a great lassitude. She was fed up with her boring marriage, her aborted affair, her limited career opportunities.

Then all of a sudden, the wind caught her. And for a moment nothing mattered anymore except making it alive to the other side of the street.

Breathing heavily, he adjusts the lens.

Ye ain't gonna see her through the walls, Claribel hisses, when ye kin barely see her through the snow.

She's out agin—where she going? He turns on her: I kin smell the booze from here! Don't switch the lights off, she seen us already!

I didn't switch no light off, Claribel says.

The rooms behind them have disappeared. The glows from neighbours' windows. The street lamps. Only the snow remains. Only the storm. Only Dolora's figure struggling across the street.

Fabian knows it's Angéline calling, it has to be. One of the two slim men in tight pants in the next apartment will answer, they can never resist answering. She'll recognize the voice and say hello, will you please check in on my husband, he's sick. A lie of course, two lies: he's not just sick, he's dying. And he's not her husband.

Someone knocks on the door. Someone pounds, shouts, piercing the concentration he must maintain to keep the pain at bay. He recognizes the voice, he hears it receding: there's nobody in there. Oh but there is, there is. More pounding.

He shouts: go away, but all they can hear is his cry of pain. I'll get the janitor, he has a pass key.

There's a commotion in her real husband's house at the

same moment. On the phone, a whisper: you think you can come back? And in the doorway, a blotched face, the smell of alcohol, followed by two policemen enormously dark among the pale furniture. They carry in a stretcher. She finds sweaters, a sleeping-bag, comforters to wrap the boy. The girl starts to wail: don't go! Don't go away again Mommy! The father glares: you might as well stay now you're here. I can't, he's dying. He's not dying, he's got appendicitis—I mean Fabian, she says: Fabian's dying. And she falls on her knees, no that's too much, she just stands there. She says, very quiet: if you'll take me down the hill on the snowmobile with you now, I'll come back afterwards, I'll take care of the house and kids, give me a few days and I'll be your maid forever, I'll work for you free. Like hell you will, he barks! The house goes pitch black. The children scream. Like all bloody hell, he barks again, his voice, slurred and malevolent and disembodied in the dark.

The redhead in a green dress has lit a cigarette. Windows on that side of the building face an inner courtyard where snow falls more vertically because the wind can't gather momentum. She feels a little flushed, and pushes the window up an inch. A small gust of uncommonly pure air rushes in. But the light wavers. She turns around to find candles.

What surprises her when the power fails is not the darkness so much as the silence. Her radio faltering in mid-sentence. The fridge not humming anymore. The humidifier not sighing. The television sets mute beyond the walls.

She shuts the window. You don't squander heat in a power failure in winter. She sticks a couple of candles in empty wine bottles and crosses the shadowy hall, and pushes a door. I brought you a candle, she says, isn't there a doctor upstairs? Yeah, one of them answers. A bloody Ph.D. She doesn't dare ask what's a Ph.D., and why can't he help anyway since he's a doctor?

Fabian moans. Angéline presses her face on the glass of the door. The blizzard swallows the snowmobile caravan with her husband, the two policemen and the sleigh they're pulling behind them, in which they've laid down her son.

Lois has almost arrived. A glitter of headlights embroiders the snow. The city blazes like a birthday cake under too much icing. She doesn't know she's catching the last elevator to reach the top of the Complex before the power failure. She doesn't realize how scared she should be, or how grateful.

I'm Dolora. Removing her boots. Putting on some shoes, which she takes out of her coat pockets. Pulling off her hat, her hair shimmering like cock feathers in candlelight. Nodding at a shadow who limps closer, his cane in one hand, a candle trembling in the other. They don't usually pay attention to him the old fart, I'll bet she's seen him in the window with his binoculars.

Ye're not the one who phoned.

No I was afraid you'd refuse.

Imagine the police finding me with the Mayor's wife, they'd stick me in jail forever.

They'd have to stick me in with you. And she laughs, sounding like fingers running over the high notes of a piano.

He shivers, realizing he's lived across the street from her for years, waited hours on end day after day for just a glimpse of her, and never once heard her laugh, never knew what he missed. Now he'll know. Now he'll miss it.

The wind shoves the house. We're like the three little pigs in here, Claribel says, sinister.

She'll be boasting tomorrow. She'll be boasting for years. Our neighbour the Mayor? Eh, heh, heh, heh! There he was passing laws against fortune-tellers, and all the time his wife was a client of mine!

9

The stairwell was crowded like an aisle after a movie. Ten thousand people work in this building, Blanche said. That's three times the population of my hometown, Noel said. Oh yeah? Way down river, not far from the Gulf; by the way, do you know what Blanche means? She nodded, smiling. And he stared at her teeth, and at an emergency light, reflected twice in her obsidian eyes.

The stairs zig-zagged from landing to landing. Were they ever meant to carry such a crowd, he wondered? She stumbled and he steadied her, spanning her waist with his hands.

Further up, he caught her hand and shuddered at the contact of the nails, like stilts on her fingers. How do you manage to do any typing? Oh, we all have electronic keyboards.

The crowd flowed in both directions. He touched her nails again. You some kind of witch? You scared of witches? Scared doesn't meant I don't like them. And his lips brushed her very soft cheek. And she turned, and he felt on his own cheek the surprising roughness of her hair, and again on his lips the surprising softness of her skin, and then the bottomless sweetness of her mouth.

You're late. She's ensconced in a corner of the bar, five flights up from the office. Unlike the stairs, the bar gets no light from the emergency generator. But even in candlelight, Boris sees that she's drunk, and wishes Jack were here. I took the last elevator up that didn't get stuck, she says.

You're drunk, he says.

She lifts her glass: to all the people stuck in all the elevators—

Come on let's eat.

She protests.

She waves away the menu.

Boris orders.

Shall I send you the wine steward, Sir?

Glowering: Christ, use your judgment.

Lois hums.

People stare.

Boris asks: would you rather eat in the office?

You ashamed of me?

You bet I am.

I suppose you'll get even once we're home, but that won't be for a long time. *Un bel di vedremo,* she sings.

You'll be sorry, Lois.

She grins. Alcohol coats her with a thin sugary glaze which he, Boris, is of course a master at cracking. What about all those people stuck in elevators? Do we leave them there? Like Aïda in her tomb?

Spare us the recital.

I don't suppose you care.

He says plaintively: I'm glad you got the part.

She slams her water glass down on the table, splashing the bread in the bread basket: you're lying!

But patrons are turning away to a more novel distraction at the door.

My, but this place hops—hey! where you off to? Slow down!

There are thumps and a loud murmur. A crash near the entrance. The maître d' asks for a napkin, blood trickling out of his nose. Noel gets up from the floor. They hit him first, Blanche explains, they won't let us in because he isn't wearing a tie. Boris grimaces, morose: how could you let this happen? Blanche is offended. Lois appears behind Boris and intervenes with a mischievous grin: why don't you two join us? Blanche declines. Noel accepts. Boris sighs and leads the way back to the table. A waiter adds two chairs, two settings. Lois sits between the men across the table from Blanche. Boris says: the bread is wet. Lois turns to Noel: I'll bet you eat like a horse, and look at you: not a grain of fat; and what do you do for a living? I wash windows. On a day like today—my, my, but Boris is all heart, isn't he? Inside windows, Mrs. Leduc, Blanche points out. Mr. Masson washes the windows inside the building. Call me Noel, Noel says. Me too, Lois, says, I mean call me Lois. Boris doesn't chime in. Calling him Boris would be the last straw.

Everyone rose to greet the Mayor. The Vice-President of the Council pushed toward him on the table a list of items already discussed in his absence and ratified. Minor ones. Victor Demers ratified with his initials each ratification: VPD. He'd changed his middle name from Isidore to Pierre, preferring the latter's association with the rock foundation of Christianity to a middle I which, between V and D (as if VD weren't bad enough) spelled phonetically "void" in French. He'd often wished his parents, so prophetic in their choice of a name, had paid a little more attention to the initials. His phone rang. It was acknowledged with affection among committee members that the quickest way to reach the Mayor when you sat across the table from him, was to dial his number. Circuits were overloaded, citizens requested, over the radio, to confine their telephone calls to urgent matters. There's no new business anymore but weather reports, Mr, Mayor, a stationary storm track...clusters of storms which should have been scattered...

Contact the heads of all grocery chains with warehouses within a radius of twenty miles, Victor ordered. Our first priority must be to provide food for people stranded inside our city limits.

Across the river, Jack had explained to the children that they were safe, they were the ones who'd made it home and didn't have to share their provisions—

We've got to share with you, one of the children said tartly.

Edith murmured: there's plenty…

And no heat to cook on!

There's a fireplace, lots of firewood…

I'll bet you forgot extra batteries for the radio, Mrs. Hobart!

You're a nit-picker like your father, she snapped. But he was right. She had.

Jack found the boy the spitting image of Lois, not Boris. He knew better, however, than to mention Lois now. He'd been inching his way closer on the sofa for the past half-hour, warming up the cushions underneath him as he went. Edith hadn't noticed. Or pretended she didn't. She was acting vague, unfocused.

All of a sudden she turned on him. Their eyes met. Or rather, collided. She startled him by blaring out: now don't go getting any ideas, buster!

Silence fell like a knife, leaving him flayed and tremulous. He sensed stares converging from every corner of the room. Anybody ever goes to bed around here, he bellowed in retaliation? Go ahead, whisper among yourselves, see if I care!

I was only saying I was scared, a small voice wailed.

Edith poured herself another drink. She'd had too much already, the bottle trembled on the rim of the glass.

The storm pawed the windows, tugged on the eaves, threw an arm over the roof and blew down the chimney.

At home, Dolora slept in a room of similar dimensions, in a bed the same size, and on barely friendlier terms with the man she shared it with. Seated across Claribel on a cheap "sateen" bedspread, she stared at the cards fanned out between them, amazed anyone could decipher such greasy, half-erased faces, and in candlelight to boot.

They've talked in their day, Claribel began, sensing scepticism. Claribel came into her own the minute she touched her instrument. She appeared all of a sudden perceptive and articulate. Compassionate and knowing. I'm not like other fortune-tellers who'll just read your mind, she said. I don't even need cards if it came to that. She fingered a dark King: love.

That, Dolora thought, is what she tells everybody, or I wouldn't be here.

A man alone, Claribel continued. You may not be free, but he is. You haven't had love in a long time. Even when you had it, it didn't make you happy. And yet the Mayor loves you in his way. He loves you more than you love him: that's pretty clear to me, the way he tries to take your arm when he walks you to that big car in the morning, and the way you—you never let him.

You don't understand—

Eh, heh. I understand. Love for you is someplace else. A man your husband hardly knows. A man in your line of work maybe—do you work? Don't tell me. You do, though. There's something you do, and somebody you do it with—

Dolora gazed at the fortune-teller, wondering if people like her (or for that matter: who, apart from artists themselves) ever read the Arts section of a newspaper.

That man, Claribel continued, that dark man I'm talking about, you just saw him. Maybe yesterday or even today when you went off in the morning and never came back until four in the afternoon. Don't tell me but you know I'm right. She faltered. It's not a happy love. Why are you cold with him? I'm right, aren't I? Of course I'm right, but shh. Listen. Listen to that storm up there.

And the two women cocked their heads.

It's a killer, mark my words. And grim, she tapped another card. Death, she said. That man, you see...that dark King...he likes things that's bigger than life.

Dolora stifled a smile, remembering the size of Terence's models.

He likes going too far, he's attracted to danger, and even, Claribel faltered: let's face it, death is as far as anybody can go. He has other women because he can't have you. But with you, he could go too far, he could love too much. You think he'd bed you down and walk away but he wouldn't. He thinks about it, and so do you, so why is it when the two of you are together it's like you're not talking the same language? Why, Claribel asked, why do you turn away?

Angéline had appeared in a corner of the room with a child on her lap, tears plopping out of her eyes onto her sweater, her hands, rolling between the child's fingers, large live tears like crystals on a chandelier when a breeze blows in from a window—

The redhead fidgets. She craves a smoke. She feels the pack in the pocket of her green robe.

It's pretty in here, she reflects, and glances down at the sick man with a mixture of curiosity and squeamishness. He must have been handsome, once. Nice hands. Good teeth. It's just the eyes give you the creepies the way they stare right past you. She has a cousin, a nurse, says when they get that faraway look, they don't have much longer.

He struggles weakly toward the drawer of the bedside table. She opens it for him. With a pang she sees the syringe. His clammy fingers are on her wrist. She blurts out: what do you want?

The two slim men from down the hall have tiptoed in behind her. That's morphine, one of them says, the younger one. How do you know? Believe me, I know. Should we give it to him? He's high already, can't you tell?

The redhead taps the window to dislodge gobs of snow

from the glass. Listen, I gotta get some air.

She opens the door.

She feels the hall growing colder. She hears the quiet. She hears the instinct of silence darkness has brought on.

I wish it had a mind.

A what?

The storm, Blanche says. I wish I could go out there and say: hey Mister Storm, would you be good enough to stop?

Boris looks up sourly: what makes you think it would listen? Look at her (nodding at Lois): you think she'll stop if I ask her? You think she doesn't love doing it even more if I say stop?

Doing what, Lois asks, contemptuous: what are you talking about?

Christ, who cares.

Glassy-eyed, she hums. She hasn't had a drink in hours. She's fading, while the rest of the room is getting drunker and higher.

Boris notices how easily she can ignore him. Quite an art she has perfected, there. He hates her with all the force of his long-thwarted love. He sees her naked. He sinks his teeth into her white neck. He pulls on her uncoiled hair. He punches her smeared mouth hard enough to pierce the lip, cut the tongue. Pow. And pow again. And while gathering his fist under the table, he tugs on the tablecloth, his glass falls and breaks on the edge of his plate. He has a flash of sobriety: I'm drunk.

Blanche starts. Noel stares.

Lois deigns to emerge from her *rêverie:* King Klutz rides again, she murmurs. Anywhere else she could be getting drunk all over again, but not here. Their jobs are at stake, the cowards.

Boris orders another liqueur.

He praises it, hoping she lusts for one. She likes Amaretto, albeit for its Italian name, which she delights in translating incorrectly: A Little Love, she calls it. He watches her through the liquid in the tiny glass, as if it afforded a secret and novel view of her. He sees her as the girl in the song who asked the lover she didn't love: bring me your mother's heart for my dog. And he did. And she would. He wouldn't put it past her to be true to a song like that.

When Blanche announces softly that a building seems to be on fire somewhere across the Plaza, Boris surfaces as if from a nightmare.

Hey, Lois says. Where you going?

He turns away, afraid of the violence still viable enough inside him to send her reeling.

Did you hear me, she cries, startled? Where do we meet afterwards?

We don't, Boris answers, making a dash for the door. I've had it with you. Go out and sing—do what you have to, make a fool of yourself—

What's he saying? How do I get home? When will you be back, Boris, she shouts? Hey! You can't take off just like that! Come back here, Boris! Come back here right this minute or I'll sing! I mean it, Boris, I'll sing!

Fabian knows he's awake. He feels the lead-heavy cold of the room, the airless dark, the storm sitting on his chest. He notices every lump in the mattress, and knows that was how she knew, the Princess and the Pea: she was dying.

He smiles weakly. He can still escape. He can still make short excursions into lack of pain. But never far enough, a part of him is always caught behind, a foot in a trap, a coat-tail in a door. And he can no longer muster the effort it takes to feel lucky for no violence and no surprises: that doesn't work anymore, the power's gone, someone whispers.

A woman joins them, also holding a candle: green arms, a green belt, great big green tits. She pulls a chair near the bed.

65

You can leave, she tells the other two. Fabian shuts his eyes, trapping people in elevators all over the city, in the lobbies of public buildings while snow climbs above doors and windows, in metro stations by piling snowdrifts against the exits, and more people in pitch-black trains where they can at least sit down and produce a few matches and lighters, and after a while pull out of their bags something to eat and something to wash it down with. Hey, this is fun, a woman says, offering corn-flakes like peanuts to her fellow travellers. But tomorrow she'll refuse to share the rest of her groceries, they'll have to take it by force, they'll eat the cartons and the bags, anything they can chew on. The tunnels will be locked by then. Ventilation will have stopped working.

Fabian gasps. The wind shakes the house, gluing its lips to the windows and chimneys, sucking all the air. The woman in green runs into the hall: you gotta give him his fix, I'm not doing it, not me, I don't know how!

He free-falls into lack of pain. Only after a while does he see light at the bottom, landing into the thick, soapy fury of the blizzard on Angéline's heels, hearing what she hears, fragments of sound on the wind—a cry, a car's horn. But when he shouts her name, he sees it bouncing off a cover the wind has spun over her.

Who's Angéline? the green woman asks; and the sound of her own voice embarrasses her. She stands up. His lips move in his dream. She walks over to the window thinking she'd have liked a window on the street herself, you'd at least know what was going on. She turns back and bumps into the desk. Imagine making up stories at his age, and pictures in the margins if you please, a black woman making love to a white man, the two of them in their street clothes, her boots wrapped around his windbreaker. Christ. Takes all kinds. She raises the candle:

...which the redhead had supplied when the power failed;

and they remembered a little guiltily how they had found her vulgar, and that they'd called her The Irish Tart because she wore green almost all the time.

10

The phone rings. Terence almost doesn't answer. Smoke is already seeping into the studio. Thin tentacles curling around the mural that should have been delivered over a week ago. Small billows almost invisible, almost odourless, which in half an hour will thicken, and hang there.

She says his name in the voice of his daydream. Is she his daydream, or does she only fill a gap?

He stands up. He clutches the phone against his chest as if it were she, as if he could hold her. He doesn't tell her one of the old townhouses in the row where he lives, where she worked with him hours ago, has caught fire. You know what that means, Dolora? Fire engines can't get through, the storm is barring the way, nothing can move, my studio's doomed. He doesn't mourn the tall graceful windows whitewashed with snow, which will be charred by morning. He doesn't grieve for his chilly, spacious rooms, bound to become an inferno before the night is over. He doesn't tell her he can already see the sparks among the snowflakes. That a black torrent of melted snow is cutting channels into the white dunes of the Plaza. That he won't save anything except her mural, and a jewel-like portrait he once made of her from memory, endowing the eyes with a look of love he doubts anyone has ever seen in them.

She blames the strangeness of his voice on the scene

between them earlier. She launches into an ill-timed promise, cooing she wants what he wants. She hears herself sounding contrived, she cringes, she trails off.

Instead of rescuing her, he asks: why now? Why do you say this now? Could she make the rest not matter? Other tenants have just begun to drag their possessions down the long, curved stairs. He asks: so what has Victor done to you, that you must use me for revenge?

Done, she says? Nothing, he's snowed in at City Hall. You won't believe this but I'm at a fortune-teller's across the street from home. I'm told there's death in my cards, death in this storm, I want to talk to you because—who knows if there'll be a tomorrow?

Ah, he says bitterly. so if there'll be no tomorrow, if there'll be no chance of my collecting what you promise, what do you risk, phoning me now?

She isn't prepared for his objection. She hasn't rehearsed a counter-argument. She didn't for a minute imagine she'd have to plead with him. According to her scenario, he should have believed her with alacrity and utter gratitude.

Lois hangs up. Edith tells me her husband's stuck in a bar someplace but Jack's still there, where else— The bitch. Noel squeezes her hand: the three of us got to stick together, Lois, we'll be all right if we do, won't we, Blanche? Blanche says yes, but she'd rather the two of them than the three of them. Noel glows after so many cognacs. On the stairs between the Panorama Restaurant and the office, and while still holding onto Lois' hand, he pauses to savour Blanche's lips, to lick her perfect teeth, to wonder if he's already asked are they real and what she answered, and whether it matters.

The office seems cavernously dark after the busy stairwell. Lois stares down at the red glow outside, which disappears and reappears in the cauldron of the storm. Will Boris be glad to see those old houses razed. He has no use for old houses, a blight on modern cities, he calls them: rat-infested and insalubrious. Would you believe, Lois says to Blanche, my husband actually uses words like that in normal conversation: insalubrious?

She burps, hating Boris as if the fire and the snow were his fault and his tools.

A bell tolls, an alarm from the cathedral steeple, which the wind waves into its huge, continuous roar. The glass walls vibrate. You think they'll hold? They're unbreakable, Noel reassures her. This is a very solid building, Mrs.Leduc, Blanche chimes in. Call me Lois, Lois says. Ah yes, Lois, Blanche says.

They sit on the floor. They use their overcoats as blankets. Lois dozes off.

Blanche's impossibly long eyelashes flutter on Noel's temple. What he wants to ask is: are you real, all of you, and never mind the teeth, the nails, the eyelashes. He explores the broad and deep inside of her mouth. The sea of sweetness of her lips.

He sees himself back in his village, entering church on a Sunday, his mother on one arm, Blanche on the other. He sees the astonishment of the congregation, the disbelief, the craning of necks. His imagination takes a step backwards. To the moment when he and Blanche get off the bus at the depot, and take a taxi home, and pay, and get out, with the dog barking in the front yard, and the Virgin Mary open-armed in her grotto in an old bathtub, and his mother waiting on the threshold, holding the door ajar. Mother I want you to meet— Mother I want you to meet— Mother I want you to meet— The record has a crack, he gives it a small push: the girl I'm going to marry. And he shivers with all the terror of his old prejudices.

Are you cold, Blanche asks?

Me too, Lois murmurs.

The storm nudges the glass walls. The storm has a thousand arms, a thousand voices. And Lois, lulled by the wind, heaves on the waves of the lovers' love.

Jack had studied the floor plan while Edith put the kids to bed: the master bedroom was the last door off the hall. Light from the fire didn't reach as far. He poured her another drink. She extended a hand to take it. He backed away, forcing her to stand up and follow. Groping for her glass, she touched him instead. He eluded her. She lunged. He dropped the glass, wetting her feet and ankles. Edith, I hurt you! I'll live, she said. They helped each other up. They struggled in the dark like a pair of silent dancers. He fastened onto her warmth. The fire crackled minutely. The storm tore at the roof. Jack heard himself sobbing. Her lips tasted of scotch. Hold me, Edith, he whispered. Hold me.

Where are those food trucks!

They can't get through, Mr. Mayor. Ah, and there's been looting. Not just food, but electronic equipment, Sir. Jewellery.

Goddamit with all the guards I've hired!

Guards are freezing to death on their feet, Sir, fires burning out of control all over the city—but don't worry, none on your street, Mr. Mayor, I've checked.

Issue a warning, for crying out loud! Tell people to be careful with their goddam candles!

He sits down. A brief silence greets him. A clearing of throats. For a moment there is more fear of the Mayor's temper than of the storm that whistles down the fireplace.

Victor turns to look at it. No-one has ever thought of buying wood for the fireplaces of City Hall. No-one even knows if they work or were ever meant to. They must: a protuberance on the wall shows that there are actually flues that go up to the roof.

Maybe, Mr. Mayor, one of the Councillors suggests while they get into the liquor supply—but it isn't enough, it warms up the gut but not the toes—maybe we could burn a few of those old boardroom chairs we used to have in here before we voted for new ones.

Later, a little drunk, Victor keeps a vigil while his Councillors sleep with their heads on the boardroom table. How well arranged for burning is the wood of a chair, he reflects, with plenty of air between the legs, and the seat perpendicular to the flames as they rise. But there should have been many more, someone's been delving in the supply, someone who has a right of entry to the storerooms, who has keys, duplicates, opportunities—someone he trusts goddamit is there no end to these iniquities!

Indignation flares in him. It illuminates every reason he's ever had for resentment. It ignites a huge, impotent rage. He stares at the snow-blinded windows, at the turbulence outside. He raises his fist. Why, he rasps? Why?

A grunting response came from the toilet. The old man knew the house and he could corner Dolora, even with a bad limp, even without light. Help, she cried! And Claribel grunted, in a deadlock with her bowels. Help, I mean it! Dolora shouted again. And the old man charged, holding his cane in front of him like a sword, trying to jab and stab and impale her. She hopped up on the table. She wailed in outrage: why are you doing this? What have I done to you?

Done? he hollered. Ye're as bad as the worsta them! Propositioning yer boyfriend right under my very nose! I been telling Claribel this second Flood's becausa the womin! Becausa them cheating on the poor buggers who break their backs trying to please them!

A flashlight scanned the room: what tha hell's going on!

Dolora gasped. The cane was not all that the old man had been brandishing.

Well if that ain't a rare sight! Claribel bellowed. If that ain't an urge that's survived its usefulness! She grabbed the cane.

He doubled up, turned around, scampered.

But the blows rained: ye won't be hard to bury! I'll push ye out the door! They'll find ye in the spring!

He'd lost his footing, he was a crumpled, whining, wheezing heap on the floor. But she continued to beat on him as if she were putting out a fire, which, in a sense, she was.

Dolora jumped off the table. All right, enough, all we need is a corpse in here!

Claribel turned on her. We don't need ye either. Go home.

As if I could go home, Dolora said. As if I could get out the door, let alone across the street.

Read this.

He picks up the manuscript. He shakes his head. Hey, he summons his friend.

They read aloud together. They laugh, the two of them. The girl laughs along with them. But then she asks: is it true you call me The Irish Tart?

They deny it passionately. (Of course, it's true: the sick man must have overheard them.) They don't bother ask her whether she ever calls them names. They know she does as often as she has anybody to call them names to.

She chooses to believe them, and to believe they've never felt despised or ridiculed by her. She listens to the storm's huge breath outside, while inside, the sick man's tenuous respiration fills the room.

It seems incredible to Terence that he once had the temerity to will all this to a museum, and then the lesser audacity to leave it to Dolora, to put her in charge of his Immortality—to hope that gratitude would motivate her, if admiration didn't. Now if he has one regret, it is that she will never see the many portraits he has painted of her.

There is a semblance of humanity in portraits. Whenever he must destroy one, he turns it around, he can't bear the look in the eyes while he slashes the canvas. By the same token, he will leave the door ajar in the hope of speeding up their annihilation, of sparing them pain.

He's untacked the mural from its frame and rolled it into a tube. He wraps the jewel-like portrait of Dolora in a soft undershirt and slips it inside his coat before walking out.

When he looks back, the dark empty house seems to have lost consciousness before the approach of the fire.

There is a sound of exploding glass.

He wouldn't be far from dead by now. Asphyxiated. It doesn't take long.

Someone bars his way, some self-important small shot, there's one on the scene of every disaster: hey you with the carpet, where do you think you're going? Terence faces him squarely: who are you? The man shouts above the wind that he's the manager of the complex across the plaza.

Terence pushes the tube in his arms. Here. I saved your mural.

Christ, Boris says, what do I want with this now?

But Terence is gone, and from a distance, watches the flames engulfing his home, the work of his lifetime, fed, enlivened by paints, turpentine, solvents, canvas, oil soaked rags, by the fabrics and dried flowers he used as backgrounds, by the screens behind which his models undressed, by the old wooden platform on which time and time again over the years he's bedded them before they put their clothes back on. He thinks of all the times when he's vainly wooed greatness in his work and in love. He's had a rich life—rich in anything he didn't value. But what he really longed for, he never attained.

He walks around the crowd toward the last townhouse. Tenants are still scurrying out, tossing their possessions from the windows. I've got to get back in, he shouts at a man who would restrain him, another one. You can't go in there! My daughter! he shouts. The other steps aside. He rushes in, with Dolora's portrait on his chest under his coat. Again on the stairs someone intervenes, but he's found a powerful password and people scramble out of his way. There's nobody left in there, they shout! Oh yes there is, but don't come up, I'll manage! They're only too glad to be excused from following.

He detects under the smell of smoke a familiar whiff of paints. He stalks it. He enters a studio, bumps into an easel that he recognizes by touch and continues past it, to a rack against a wall, his hands encountering canvases stacked on their sides on the floor. He wishes he had a light by which to judge whether they deserve to be lost as his own. He feels a rush of empathy for the humility of the painter: did he save anything else, a watch, a cat, or is he stuck somewhere, unaware of the fire?

Terence hears boots on the stairs. Young men's voices, no doubt some of the volunteers the Mayor's hired to help since the storm began.

He crouches under an inverted V between two large canvases. He rearranges them so the front sides touch and close. He feels the roughness of a painter's sheet underneath him. He smells the varnishes and solvents. He holds Dolora's portrait high on his chest, imagining her lips on his nipples.

The voices enter the room.

Not a chance.

Even if the wind changed directions?

Dry old buildings…

They're near enough to touch. Their flashlights throw flying saucers on the ceiling. They shout: anybody in here? They mention a trap-door to the roof, probably weighed down by tons of snow. Why would he go out that way? Well like I said, I never saw him come out.

Terence holds his breath. A beam scans the room. Someone strikes a match, they're going to leave him a candle, he'll be able to appraise those canvases after all before smoke and fire obliterates them. Hey! What did you do that for! Building's burning anyway! Better get outa here!

A rumble of descending feet. He jumps up. He sees the flame on the drip sheet before it engulfs him, before he bursts into light, before all his past flashes like an overexposed film, the memories of time lost searing him. He hears himself screaming, and another part of himself realizing this is the price he must pay for escaping old age, a drawn-out death, the acknowledgement of failure, lack of love, loneliness. This is the price, this hideous moment when he's a fireball in a fire-filled room.

The crowd roared. The wind lifted the sound like a retching. The last in the row of townhouses was burning out of turn, fire jumping over two buildings on its path. In a front room of that furthest house, a shadow had materialized, staggered, crashed through a window and fallen like a flaming comet. Aghhh, roared the crowd with horror and relish. And it closed ranks on the mass that shrivelled like tar, like toffee, the snow hissing on him. As soon as he was cool enough, they searched his charred pockets. Hey! Boris said. We got to identify him! Leave him alone! He won't miss nothing now. Boris walked away and was sick. His vomit made a small steaming fjord in the snow. He washed his mouth with more fresh snow, wondering what was in it that he didn't see, what filth ready to be scooped up if he were to disturb the surface. The large tubular parcel trembled in the wind. The mural. The Mayor's wife's, already half-paid for. He picked it up and put it in the arms of a bystander. Ta hell with this, I'm a free man. He felt light and sleepy. A block away from the fire, it was as if nothing were happening, he might have reached the South Pole, he was alone with the unreasoning fury of the storm. He longed to sleep. He considered sitting down, giving in. But the lonely cunning of such a death terrified him. He read a street sign and altered his direction. He tried to force open the door of a shop. The people stuck inside, in the dim light of a candle, rounded their eyes and moved their lips like fish in an aquarium. A snowmobile almost ran him over. Don't you know there's a curfew! I know! he shouted, I only want to sleep!

He gave them the address of Jack Niccolini's apartment.

II

Now pain is in control, pain nails him to the bed. Every movement, every small effort even of raising an eyelid, every breath, every tick of the heart triggers the pain. He weeps her name tearlessly, wondering even now whether it's the best name for her, now that he's reached the worst part of dying, the limit of what he can endure before the cables begin to snap.

The rattle stops. She panics. Oh shit don't let him die while I'm alone with him! He breathes again, the rattle weaker, caught in a wheel that's turning too slow.

She puts the paper back on the pile and picks up the candle. She feels the sick man watching, she's not sure. There's movement on the bed, a rustling. She opens her mouth to explain: I just wanted to see what kinda work it is you do. But the door creaks and another candle enters the room, so she says nothing.

Fabian sees all these eyes, all these moist openings floating above him like small wet balloons. Someone whispers as if he didn't exist, as if his illness deprived him of his hearing:...only one left, do we give it to him now, or do we wait?

And he's back in the bowels of the metro, the platform pitch black. The trains in the tunnels pitch black. The stairs, the stations up the stairs, the deadly crushing crowds at the exits.

Then he's outside in a heaving white darkness, with the cold grit of snow on his teeth.

He's dead.

Dolora picks up the receiver. You're right.

I don't mean that.

The old man switches off the radio. We gotta save the batteries.

Won't be no point turning it on, Claribel snaps, when there's nobody left at the other end! She flicks the switch back on. A distant voice sputters: meteorologists baffled...citizens leaving shelters at the peril of their lives...People trapped in single-storey buildings...

That's us, he says. Single-storey building. That's us.

Dolora thinks of her daughters who never made it home from school but stayed downtown, thank God, there is no street here anymore, snow has buried the windows.

She turns on Fabian. She comes at him as he lies barely breathing on the bed: you can't do this to me, I haven't lived, I can't end up dying between these two spiteful nobodies!

Go away, Fabian sighs. But she grabs him, shakes him by the shoulders; I'm not going! Not until you bring him back! I don't care what you do to the others—kill them all off if it makes you feel better, but not him and not my children and not me!

Me too, Lois says. I don't want Jack alone with that woman.

Get her husband in there on the double.

Fabian's laughter fills the room like a flutter of moths.

When the power failure had trapped Edith Hobart's husband in the metro, he'd walked the last stretch of tunnel to the south shore station, and then tried to continue on foot above ground. But after half a block he was so cold, he couldn't feel his hands and feet, so he stumbled into a bar and drank just long enough to blur his notion of danger.

He tried again, and this time, tackled the milestones one by one. If I can only cross the parking-lot, for instance. If I can only see the fence, and find the gate. Next: the cautious crossing of the street over the buried stream of traffic. Beyond it a bar where he could warm up. The remaining few blocks were a cinch. Neighbours all the way. He could stop anywhere. Or so he thought. He hadn't taken into account that all their doors were stuck and buried. He was too drunk to check or to care.

He forced open the master bathroom window. It was higher than the rest, still above the snow level, and fitted with a flimsy latch. He'd gone in that way once before, one night when Edith was mad and wouldn't let him in. He landed with one foot in the toilet. Never mind, he had his boots on. He took them off. His frozen clothes leaned on the wall. Edith, he burped, I'm home.

He wriggled into bed. Move over, Edith, give a guy a little room, willya? He kissed the back of the neck. An elbow fended him off. Come on, Edith. The form turned around. Embraced him. Glued its lips to his, groaning, groping for the crotch.

It must have encountered something unexpected.

It started and sat up: what tha hell!

Edith stirred, turned around, sat up and then yelled.

The children ran in with flashlights from the back of the house.

Boris of course had a key—why be barred from the den of his own wife's temptation? He'd secretly had a copy made of Lois' copy—the one Jack had given her before he went to Italy. And now he counted the flights, remembering to count the landings.

The long, narrow hall felt as cosy as the inside of a coffin. Imagine living in a place like this, among traffic noises and the odours of other people's cooking, and that parody of nature: the cramped city balcony with its rhapsodic luxuriance of potted coleus—and deadly martinis.

He read the metal number on the doors like braille. He fitted the key in the lock. It took him two hands to do so.

A familiar scent rushed him. Douses himself like a woman, the prick.

He remembered candles in candlesticks on a credenza, never lighted, never growing shorter, only a duller and dustier shade of blue. Matches in an onyx box on the fake mantelpiece.

The bathroom was down the hall. He shook his coat over the tub, and hung it there to dry after assuring himself there was no longer any hot water for a bath. He considered using Jack's toothbrush. He settled for rubbing a dab of toothpaste on his teeth with his forefinger. He undressed but kept on his underwear, which still had on it the last of his body heat. He added a sweater from Jack's drawer—cashmere, the bastard. Soft thick socks. He set the candle on the bedside table. He wriggled in between the tightly tucked sheets—Christ, you'd think Lois had made the bed. But he would never tell her: you and Jack have one surprising thing in common, you both make the bed too goddam tight; because if he did, she'd only rejoinder: that's because you're too goddam fat.

79

He embraced the pillow. His hand encountered something silky etched with a scratchy bit of lace, the sort of thing he liked Lois to wear, but she never did unless to go out. Why in hell now? he would ask. Who in hell's going to see them now? What if I have an accident: would you want me found in old cotton panties? Try telling her if she had an accident, he'd have other things on his mind than the style of her panties. Plus if he never saw her wearing them before, how would he know they were hers? What kind of an accident do you think I'd have anyway, she snapped: couldn't you identify me by my face? No point arguing with Lois. Don't even try.

So Jack kept women's panties under his pillow, eh? You know what kinda guy he is, Lois? You wanna know? You think he likes you? He's a drag queen, that's what. Jack Niccolini's just a bloody drag queen! The proof? Here's your proof!

A stab of recognition. That, and the way the bed was made. And the perfume trapped in the unaired rooms. And that other odour, the one in the panties, faintly sweet and sour—

He flung them away as if they had singed him. Hopped out of bed as if it were on fire.

He wanted to go home. He wanted to hide his shame in his own bed, in his own pyjamas. He wanted to tear up every picture of her, every songbook, every pair of panties plain or fancy.

But Lois inhabited him like an incurable disease. And the storm had him locked in a hold of its own.

He calls her name. It isn't a name anymore, only a long moan.

The others move back and forth across the candle, casting fractioned shadows on the pleats of the curtains.

She's on her way here, she's left home. He shuts his eyes to be with her in the white darkness of the blizzard. Objects disappear—porches, street signs, telephone booths, bus shelters. The tips of her skis graze unseen obstacles. Now and again an avalanche thunders down from an invisible gable. She must struggle against too much soft snow, too much wind that plays on her as on a sail, pushing her off course. Her clothes hinder her, yet still aren't enough. The street broadens like a river between rows of featureless buildings, no more than stalagmites with their useless doorbells and buried doorways. She raises her scarf. She can't bend her fingers.

The pain rushes partly through him, through numb limbs and loosened fingers and an indistinct mind. The cables have begun to snap.

Please! Dolora cries. The wind blows the other way! The snow will put out the fire. The children—my children—Victor sent help, they're safe—

Victor's looking for you, he says sadly. He wrote you a letter long-hand: why do you always treat me as if I hated you, Dolora?

Leave Victor, it's too late for Victor. The power's gone. Terence has lit candles. Is he still angry?

Fabian winces. He feels a trickle from the corner of his mouth. He feels the fall of his cheeks on either side of his nose.

She stands over him stubbornly. The house trembles in its quilt of snow, she says.

Yes, he says. But Terence is still angry.

She takes his hand. She kisses the palm. She slips a finger between her lips. The warmth, the life flows in from that finger, he opens his eyes, her hair billows. Give me a chance, she says, the words pulsing wetly on his finger. Time rolls backwards. They're in the studio, he's showing her that portrait of herself with the loving eyes. There's the real woman, she says, I'm just a canvas you may fill in as you please...

He begins to undress her.

You must start with the face, she says. Always. As if you loved me. And she offers her eyelids to his lips. Her open mouth. Afterwards, she guides his hand from her face to her breasts. She whispers, over Terence's shoulder: we're okay now, you can leave, this will do, thank you, go—

12

Blanche had stirred in Noel's arms. She sat up beside him. The storm waved at them from the other side of the glass, frenzied and playful. We're going to die, she said.

Don't talk like that!

We are.

Lois was up, gazing out toward the south shore. She turned on them: how are my children? accusingly, as if it were their fault. Where is my husband?

She wiped her nose with the back of her sleeve. If I get out of this alive and my family too, nothing will ever seem important again except being safe.

Yet even as she claimed this, she realized she'd salvaged her voice from the cold outside, and from the roar of the restaurant, and from the smoky stairwells, and from the dampness of the building; and that an ardent desire was in her not only to survive but to continue to sing.

Water pipes were frozen. Windows didn't open. Isn't it ironic, Lois said: trapped in here by so much snow, we're going to end up dying of thirst?

He touched an icy radiator. He tried a faucet. Knocked on a window. Gobs loosened, revealing the storm's undiminished fury. The pane wouldn't slide up, glued to the frame by frost. He'd have to break it. He must shut off one room, roll a blanket against the bottom of the door to stop the draft, and convert that room into a well, a snow mine. Never gave me credit for imagination, eh Lois? Wish you were here. Even you in this nightmare.

He imagined himself with her, growing numb and close. She might explain, seek some justification. Or even manage to forgive him. I forgive you for finding my panties under another man's pillow, dear. She'd risen to more absurd magnanimities.

There was a void in his chest as after too much weeping. He wasn't thinking of the children, it was Lois he longed for: her resilience, her energy, the tough joyous optimism she displayed all too rarely, claiming he put her in a cage. A bright garish parrot that longed to fly, Lois— You could at least make me a canary, she snapped in his head; and he chuckled and the chuckle turned into a small sob.

Even in her absence she amused him. She had this miraculous capacity that he refused to acknowledge (why?), always turning away to conceal his hilarity. You have no sense of humour, poor boring Boris. Why did he let her think that? Why wouldn't he let her know how irresistibly funny he found her?

But the children in that flimsy house—and now his concern fastened on them. Fresh tears stung his eyes. Thank God they're fat, they'll last longer. He said their names aloud. On the way to wiping his eyes, he grazed the roughness of his cheeks. He told himself: above the storm, not only on another planet, but in Toronto, in Ottawa, maybe as near as that: the sun is shining. So he shaved with thawed snow, because shaving was an expression of his appurtenance to a normal, continuing world.

Would I want Lois again under normal circumstances? Could I, after surviving this, wake up every morning to her irritation?

The wind outside whined like a violin. An icicle formed under the tap of the radiator. He broke it off and sucked on it and grimaced. It tasted of soot. He hoped it was poisonous. Poison had always seemed such a civilized exit, maybe because of that illustration in the *Petit Larousse* of Socrates serenely drinking his hemlock.

He picked up the key and opened the door into the hall. He found the tile floor a little slippery. He heard the drip of the skylight. He felt the water at his feet, drip, drip. The tenants were moving up above the snow level, arguing about time, not what time it was, but when exactly the storm had begun, how long it had been going on, when the skylight had started to drip, and when it would cave in. He turned back, mindful not to make a sound lest some of those who lived on lower floors invite themselves over. That would be the last straw. Lois, yes, but no-one else. Why is a woman a home, he wondered, and a man not?

The storm danced beyond the windows like a milkshake in a blender. He would not outlive it. He could not. He lacked the hope and the tenacity. He longed to sleep forever. To bypass any choice of an outcome.

But there wasn't enough in Jack Niccolini's bathroom cabinet to put a fly to sleep let alone a man. Not enough aspirin to cure a minor toothache. Not a half-tube of anything even remotely toxic. No piles, the bugger. Not even athlete's foot.

He'd read somewhere the fumes of ammonia could kill, but he forgot what it was you had to mix it up with. He looked under the kitchen sink. You didn't die from inhaling detergent. You had to drink it.

He forced himself to drink some. Almost immediately, he vomited. He got a pickle in the fridge to kill the taste. At home, he'd have chlordane—now how did that work? Okay then: Raid. No bugs in your coleus, Jack? No silver-fish in your old plumbing?

At last in a broom closet off the kitchen he spotted the skull and crossed bones. The oven cleaner. CAUTION. EXTREMELY CORROSIVE. His heart pounded. No that won't do.

People were arguing in the hall. He wouldn't put it past the same wanton fate, which isolated him here without barbiturates or poison, to wall in someplace else a pair of horny strangers without toothpaste or deodorant. And to compound the irony: the snow too light to walk on would end up being too heavy for the skylight.

Jack grinned from a framed photograph.

Boris' fist flew. The glass shattered. Blood gushed warmly down his fingers. Ah, he said, euphoric! Eureka! He wound a towel around his hand, picked up a large shard, wrapped it in a monogrammed handkerchief, and stashed it in his pocket. There. Like a spy with his cyanide. If Lois could see me now. Lois with her laughing incredulous eyes.

His need for her pierced him. The very memory of her flesh, of her scent, of her accursed voice, the idea of holding her once more reawakened in him an intense, an almost violent desire to survive.

Stop, he whispers, please, to the flame that pulsates to the rhythm of his pain. But they continue tiptoeing back and forth across the candle. Rustling papers. Whispering.

He kills them all off.

No, he says. But they can't hear him, they aren't listening.

He sends a storm that never ends.

Well yes but do you think they would let me?

And they stand beside the bed: what does he want? As if he were a baby.

What am I supposed to do, Edith, you think he doesn't know even if he was too drunk to remember? So why didn't you jump out of bed when the kids arrived instead of staying there with your hand on— As if I could run out stark naked and run back in and pretend I'd just arrived! Of course you had to undress, couldn't keep a stitch on in this weather, goddam continental. He sighs: you weren't complaining; and why did you have to let out this bloodcurdling scream, I mean he's just your husband, there was no need to scream your head off like that.

The children are very still, their eyes like glow-worms around the room.

They know, Edith whispers.

Of course they know, Jack says, almost shouts. She starts to cry.

Lois would be singing. She'd be telling stories. Why is it I feel you and I have been married for 25 years? Edith?

She nods at the sleeping-bag by the fire: it's hard being fun with him around.

If only we had a piano. If I'd known the storm would last so long, I'd have asked the Leduc children to let me in across the street. There's food out there. Liquor. He stares at the buried window: maybe I could dig a tunnel.

Where would you put the snow?

What snow?

The snow you'd have to take out to dig the tunnel, a tunnel is a hole!

He throws another log into the fireplace. The fire smokes. I was never good with tunnels and fires, he sighs. I'm a lover, not a bloody boy scout.

The snoring stops. The husband struggles out of his sleeping-bag. He's lost the habit of his voice. How come you and me don't fuck anymore, Edith? the husband asks out of the blue.

My father thinks you like my mother, Uncle Jack, a small voice says. Is he ever going to be happy about this.

Twit for twat, the husband mumbles.

86

After pausing to wonder what twat means (twit he remembers), Jack surprises himself by protesting. His father used to say: never admit, no matter what. So he denies. And sure enough, momentarily, the husband chooses to believe him.

Jack glances at Edith. She should be grateful instead of turning her back on them as if this conversation didn't concern her.

The husband rasps: if you hadn't put us both on a diet, Edith, we might have lived off our fat for a while.

Jack says morosely: if we get out of this with any casualties at all, they'll blame me, I suppose.

Blame you for what? Who's going to blame you?

The ones who find us. They'll blame me for anything happening to any of you. Dying of cold or hunger, or setting yourselves on fire with candles—whatever.

Are you out of your mind?

I'm the stranger here, I'm the intruder. Can you imagine your neighbours walking in and finding me alive beside the body of your husband? Or Boris Leduc finding me alive beside the bodies of his children?

Or Lois Leduc finding me alive beside your body, for that matter, Edith snaps.

13

The crowds had gone wild. When Blanche thought it her duty to unlock emergency supplies, they had grabbed all the axes, and raised them against the huge windows, and thrown themselves at the snow that blew in, and devoured it and the glass inside it, not even aware they were bleeding at the mouth.

Christ, Noel shouted, too late, arriving too late to stop the carnage, but he couldn't have. He emptied on them his repertory of invectives, while they continued to chop at random. And the wind drowned his voice and toppled the furniture. And snowdrifts began to pile up inside the building itself.

He backed away, horrified, glass crunching under his boots.

Yesterday—or was it last night, or was it this morning?—he and Lois and Blanche had moved into the Rooftop Club above the restaurant, the one scheduled to have opened just as the storm began. The three of them knew the building, and had easily recognized a small door at the top of one of the stairwells, which most people would have taken for a trap to the roof. They had arranged a bed on the carpeted platform, on a pile of cushions and tablecloths and napkins. They had slept, wrapped around one another.

But in the morning, Blanche stood up with feverish eyes and fetched a bunch of keys, and nothing would make her change her mind about going downstairs to unlock emergency supplies. It was her duty, she said. Noel couldn't stop her.

He returned upstairs. Lois unbolted the door to let him in. You can't imagine what's going on down there, he said. I wouldn't put it past them to have killed her.

He was right. She'd had to brush their hands off her face like large grey flies. Wrench their fingers off her wrists and throat. Wriggle out of their arms. Lift her knee to groins almost absent-mindedly. And when caught by her coat, untie the belt and slip away.

She found a refuge for a while in what used to be a small inner office, tucked in a nook off a partitioned section. She smelled cigarette ashes. Excrements. Her hand encountered the butt of a candle. A deck of cards spread out for solitaire.

The cards were wet, there must be a crack in the window—someone had attempted and abandoned both: the solitaire and breaking the window. The axe was still on the floor.

She built a house of cards. A thread of wind from the cracked window made it tremble and fall. She groped inside a drawer for scotch tape. She found a roll, and taped the house together, and it stood, and she felt a fine dusting of snow settling over the roof. She envisioned the tiny rooms, slowly filling up as minute drifts blew in through the spaces between the walls. The desk around her elbows grew whiter. So did the carpet around her feet. The crack must be widening, loosened by the wind. One more stroke of that axe would have done it. She slid her fingers over the glass, looking for the fissure, for the almost invisible entry of the snow. She covered it with tape. But the damp and the draft loosened the tape and it collapsed limply.

She opened the office door. Out there, windows were broken. Snow, already ankle deep. The mob had stolen her keys, not bothering to ask what else they unlocked and might have provided access to. But she had another set tucked away.

Shadows lurked and leaped. Strange cries mingled with the howling of the wind.

She found her bearings in front of an elevator. She finger-read metal indications on the wall. She followed a corridor, and at the end of that, unlocked a door and emerged into what she hoped was the appropriate stairwell.

In the swarming darkness, a flame flickered, lighting a thousand eyes. She pushed upwards. She had six flights to go. From the ground-floor of a six-storey building, that might have seemed impossible. But at this point in a skyscraper, she could tell herself she had almost arrived.

She wound her way through the moving, murmuring mass, through whispered reports of passengers asphyxiated in metro tunnels, through rumours of goons picking shopping concourses clean of cigarettes, candles, batteries, booze and of course drugs. They told my friend it was speed, one boy was saying, he died screaming, we had to throw him out a window, we threw out the guy who'd sold it to him too—

She passed a group of women. Softer bulk. Softer voices. We figured we'd be out in the morning, remember? Were you glad to get away from your old man. Someone struck a match: hey don't you work here? Me? Blanche said. Yeah didn't I see you unlocking some cabinets? The woman didn't wait for an answer. I got something for you, where are you, here! The match had gone out. Blanche found herself holding a large roll. What is it? I dunno somebody gave it to somebody who gave it to somebody who gave it to me—said it belongs upstairs.

What's upstairs, someone asked?

Nothing, Blanche lied. Just more of the same.

This snow, one women said. It's like Moira Shearer in *The Red Shoes,* remember? It can't stop. It just dances on and on and on and on and on.

She knows it's Terence's face on the pillow beside her. She can make out the moisture of his teeth and his eyes. She wants to say: I'll never go back. But that would scare him. A portable hangs on the back of a chair, spluttering. Claribel asks: you ever listen to the news like everybody else, or do they tell them to you first? I'm not here, Dolora says, didn't he tell you? Tell them, Fabian, tell them to stop bothering me!

A shadow pauses over him.

He tries to say: never mind.

The pacing has resumed back and forth across the candle. Claribel flits about the room like a fly before thunder. She pours herself another gin. The house creaks. Burps. Her old heart races, trying to cram in all the beats it's entitled to. She pities it as she would a small animal caught in a trap.

She crawls under a table. The old man cackles contemptuously. Claribel thinks: if I get out of here alive, I'm leaving him. And regret stabs her: why didn't I leave him sooner? Her eyes accustomed to darkness make out the box of the room above her, but not whether it has begun to collapse.

Won't be long now, he cackles, tapping his cane on the floor. I hope ye run outa gin first!

Not a sliver of light from outside. Not a whisper from the storm above the buried house.

You think we'll hear it before it happens?

She hears it already. The china trembling in the cupboards for the past half-hour. Doesn't he know what that means?

I'm not here, Dolora protests, frantic, I'm not here with them! The snow has stopped. The fire burned itself out because the wind blew the other way. I'm in bed with Terence. We can see Venus out the window, or Sirius, whatever, she says. What time is it anyway?

Does it matter?

Yes, if it's almost morning we wouldn't be seeing Sirius, this time of year.

He's amused: could you be seeing Venus?

If Venus were the morning star, yes. If the window faced east. Venus is in the east when she's the morning star.

They were burning all there was to burn, anything that fit into the fireplaces as they moved up above the snow level: books, magazines, shelves, old furniture, the contents of wastebaskets, every scrap of paper except toilet paper, let's not forget we're civilized, the Mayor cautioned. The liquor was finished. Drinking had numbed them for a while. Hangovers had given texture to the seamlessness of time. Now even hunger bored them. One Councillor lamented he was getting his wish too late as usual, being rid of his wife and losing weight just when there were no other women around. Another announced: I feel I'm already in that place where it said in the Bible your wife wouldn't matter anymore, you'd only have yourself to worry about... If we don't all die, a third man claimed, we'll never be normal again, they'll write about us in *Psychology Today* magazine, they'll use us to study the effect of cataclysms on humans, they'll build us a hospital, eh, Mr Mayor, they'll have to rebuild everything bigger and better than ever.

Victor found thought already diffuse and slippery. A small flame leapt in his eyes now and again, but more and more rare. He stared at the barometer in disbelief, at the needle's refusal to move to *Change*. He felt a quickening of life, thinking of Dolora. Who'd once declared eagerly in her musical voice: the tree of knowledge is science, don't you see? The apple's the bomb! We'll lose Paradise when we blow up the earth and have to inhabit a harsher planet! on Venus it's hotter than the oven when I turn it to broil! It pisses me off—she'd actually used those words: it pisses me off (he smiled)—when you call Earth a vale of tears! Try living somewhere else! For a betrayed wife, for an artist who supposedly created out of pain, Dolora had these dazzling bursts of optimism. What was she doing now, he wondered? Would she still be ready to defend her view of Earth as Paradise?

Snow covered the windows.

The councillors had hauled out the cots and mattresses used twice a year for the Mayor's blood donor clinics. Then as they climbed above the snow level, they'd abandoned the cots, they could only drag up the mattresses.

It was necessary to move again. Sighing, they roused themselves. Rooms opened up as caves along the way, each holding its separate darkness, its scoop of silence. Mattresses whispered on the floors, panted up the steps.

Each time the men emerged above the snow level, they were met with the shrill, insistent wailing of the wind.

But there's no fireplace on this floor, Mr. Mayor, someone

pointed out. We'll have to go back.

So they turned around, with their mattresses whispering behind them, panting down the steps.

After they had resettled, Victor went up alone. He wished he had a weak heart. Diabetes. He wished there were some medicine he'd have to take, or die. We should have caught typhoid all of us after the plumbing froze. We should have pneumonia by now, or at least a few colds. But look at me, I'm not even tired! Inside my gloves, my hands are still warm!

The storm swayed and screamed on the other side of the glass, its maniacal voice rising and falling.

The man of reason within him issues a last warning. Are you sure this is what you want? Are you very, very sure?

His other self answers: what I don't want is a long, lonely death. What I don't want either is what I had before.

He holds the glass at a right angle against his wrist. He presses. He feels resistance soft and rubbery—like spaghetti cooked *al dente*. The ooze tickles. Open your eyes you goddam sissy! And he does and switches hands.

Your last engine, he reminds himself. Your last chance. Hey—and weren't you going to leave a mess for the jackass?

He struggles up.

He squeezes blood out of the wound onto the pale carpet all the way to the living-room, and there, draws blood shapes on the cushions of the white sofa; hearts, crosses. He tries brushing his wrist against the wall but that hurts, so he pulls down the blood-soaked sleeve and brushes it instead around the pictures, across empty spaces, to spell fuzzy, illegible obscenities. Christ, he says aloud: I coulda painted murals myself and a helluva lot cheaper than the Mayor's wife, that pretentious twat. Love and death eh? Why not! And he draws skulls. And he draws guns, pointing at all the hearts. And he raises his candle to survey his handiwork.

He feels weak. His knees buckle, he sits on the bloodprints of the sofa. He's lost the shard, it's not in his pocket, the handkerchief's gone. He panics. The wind outside sounds almost human—a long, insane whine of derision. Jack laughs from his photograph.

Go ahead, laugh, we'll see who laughs last!

Boris pulls another shard out of the frame, a smaller one, but it will do.

The second incision is less neat than the first, his left hand inept and slippery. He feels a scraping, a tearing. Goddam butcher! His teeth chatter. He must lie down. All he wants now is a comfortable death.

The blood-spattered bed seems rumpled and uninviting. He picks up Lois' panties and smells them longingly and hangs them on a corner of the dresser mirror. There. My suicide note. There's my reason. It doesn't occur to him that Jack might not even recognize them.

He leaves the candle on the dresser and watches the roll and pitch of its reflection. The whole room sways. The unmade bed awaits him like a freshly dug grave. He doesn't want to face it so he backs off as fast as he can, until he feels the side of the mattress behind his legs.

And he falls in.

And howls.

He is sitting, impaled, on his lost shard of glass.

Are you crazy, Lois screams? Have you gone clear out of your mind? No, no, no, no! There was a woman out in the hall, didn't you see her? She and Boris met in the beam of her flashlight. All of a sudden, revenge stood there, his for the taking, in a full, fuzzy, fragrant sweater. She's followed him into Jack's apartment. They find a sterno, they make instant coffee. She asks: what's in your pocket? He shows her the shard, he tells her why. She says don't, nobody's worth that much. And he shivers as if waking from a bad dream. And they sit together on the sofa—

In all that blood!

There isn't any blood, he hasn't used the shard yet! I'll keep you warm, the woman promises. I'll pretend I'm your wife. I'll be your home for the duration of the storm. You know how it is? Lois reminds him. You said it yourself: how a woman is a home, but a man isn't?

And if you were to wake up from this nightmare? If that were all it was: a nightmare? If outside, now, it were still summer?

Jack sighs. What the hell. At this point, compliments come cheap. I'd take the first metro to the south shore, Edith. I'd ask you to run away with me.

Wouldn't you phone first?

There are things you don't ask on the phone.

I'll bet. I'll bet you've asked a thousand times and know the ropes by now. Well I don't care, nobody's ever asked me before, especially not since I got married. So I'd accept. What about Lois, though?

Porca miseria, Jack says, remembering Lois. But I think I'd want to go for the real values from now on, Edith.

Greasy prick, she murmurs, but never mind, I'm enjoying this.

Not me, the husband says. I'm not enjoying this. And he turns toward them in the dark: would you believe, Edith, I coulda been having a ball downtown but I was worried about my poor little wife all alone out here?

You were drunk, Edith says. You were always drunk. And her arms find Jack's waist in the dark. Such long arms, they're like a belt that can wind twice around him.

Later, the children snore, but just a little, as if they feared any excess might bring down the walls. I'm even scared to sleep, they whisper to one another. Me too. I'm scared of not waking up or of waking up buried. We're buried already. No I mean with snow all over my face even in my mouth and not able to breathe—

Jack throws another log on the fire. He rejoins Edith on the sofa. She's grown very quiet, her breathing sounds laboured. The husband stares from his mattress on the floor, Jack can see the fixed open eyes. The cushions are cold. I'm glad I met you, Edith, Jack says. He means that, and doesn't care who hears. His eyes smart. The children are still. Now the husband's eyes aren't visible either, maybe he sleeps.

Edith's head rolls on Jack's shoulder. Her lips move. He can't hear her clearly, he catches one word. Flu. You got the flu, Edith? No. His own chest feels tight. Her lips on his lips keep forming the same word. She nods at the fireplace.

All of a sudden, Jack understands. The flue. It's blocked up above. Air can't get in anymore. The fire is leaking smoke into the room. Consuming the oxygen.

He tries to get up. He sees something that he knows has been waiting for them. He sees it taking a step forward. He sees it looming nearer, more distinct, almost near enough to touch.

14

They'll be blaming each other, Lois weeps. They'll be telling each other: it's your fault! No yours, God sent this as a punishment for what you made me do! What do you mean, made you do? It's you who showed up at the door— Oh shut up! They'll be wondering if it hurts to be an ant crushed by a foot, they'll hide under some piece of furniture, they'll be surprised at the groaning of the walls, there'll be no power to it, no echo, no hollowness.

How do you know?

A buried house can't have great acoustics! And before it crumbles, Edith will see her whole life, and the screen on which she sees it will be Jack's sobbing back!

Noel shudders.

The children will squeal like puppies under another table—oh God! I hope they die fast! She throws herself on Noel's chest in a paroxysm of grief. She feels his tears plopping down on the top of her head. She looks up, suddenly cool: I'm telling you all this so it won't happen.

What, he asks, startled? What do you mean? What are you saying?

I mean if I imagine my children's death vividly enough, they might survive. You know how you can jinx a wish by wishing it too hard? Or spend all your anger before the person you're mad at comes home?

True, Noel says. Very, very true.

For instance, Lois says, you and I should imagine Blanche will never return. We should imagine this storm is in another time bracket like the stars, that it will stop eventually but in ten thousand years.

Aw shit! Noel starts to cry again.

Good, Lois says, that's right! You got it!

But after a night and a day (they've synchronized their watches, they've begun to keep a stricter count of time) they hear a faint knocking sound. They glue their ear to the door. Three short, three long, three short.

SOS, Lois whispers! SOS! It's Blanche!

How do you know?

Boris was in the navy!

They pull the bolt and open the door. Blanche stumbles in,

crying, sobbing, shuddering: they've destroyed everything! Axed all the windows! The storm's inside the building! Others have locked themselves in the stairwells away from the cold, but they—they're running out of air! They have no snow to eat! They're dying of thirst!

His mother is here. His father. His brother who went missing in action during the war. Death doesn't happen quickly. It happens in little leaps, little leaks. He's in and out of the final turbulence. One moment, pain has him in a vise on the bed. The next, he's in that mortal cold behind Angéline. He sees her drop a ski pole and bend down to retrieve it. He watches as the capricious wind at first heaves her up, and then hurls her downwards. He observes her astonishment. He remembers nearly drowning once, and before air hunger, before the panic of nothing to grasp and the terror of which way was up: the stillness, the terrible beckoning.

Her flaying skis arrest her fall. She clicks off a harness and ski in hand, thrashes open a passage. Sprawling not to sink in, she crawls toward some mass, some whiteness more solid than the rest. She locates a window. Through a frost coating, she can see light inside. Movement. Her frozen lips form a call for help. She blinks. Minute icicles on her eyelashes slap her cheeks.

She thrusts the back end of her ski against the glass, hard, until it cracks, explodes. She sees it flying in time, she shuts her eyes. A splinter grazes the side of her face. Large red drops fall heavily on the snow among the tiny flakes. She knocks the shards off the windowsill and raises one knee, one leg, and pulls herself in.

She lands on something soft. Glass tingles underneath her. Curtains fly. A lamp trembles and topples. The wind has extinguished the candle. The room is dark. But the storm blows in and slowly bleaches everything.

She catches sight of a figure in an armchair across the room.
She starts: have you been here long?
I was waiting for you.
How did you get in?
He nods at the window: I had to break my own.
She understands. She stands up without unfolding her
legs, without disturbing or ringing the glass underneath her.
She stands up with the ease of a gust of wind.

The storm was no longer alive. It couldn't help its fall, or pick
itself up. It couldn't move on. The clouds from which it fell
were dead.

On top of the tallest structure, the man and the two
women made music. They invented stories, which they took
turns at scribbling on drink chits. They unrolled and propped
up against a wall with chairs the three panels of the mural
Blanche had received in the stairwell. They contemplated it,
and tried to interpret its meaning in the light of candles placed
at different spots across the room.

Boris would have hated it, Lois said smugly. But as time
wore on, she wasn't so sure.

They'd found thousands of canapés, which they kept fro-
zen by storing them alongside the glass walls. They had nuts,
chips, pretzels, olives, pickled onions, mints, chocolates.
They drank mixers and beer.

They tried to keep track of time even though they'd lost
count of it somewhere in the beginning.

Then one morning, or maybe one afternoon, after sleep,
they recognized a sharper quality to light before they even
opened their eyes. They sat up. They thought they saw a blue
flag unfurled against the glass. They thought the snow had
turned blue. They thought they were dreaming or dead. They
couldn't believe it was a clear sky that they saw.

The pilot wondered: why do you figure they broke all the windows?

Several helicopters had been sent out in the beginning. Most had turned around before crossing the river. A few had lost their way. Others ventured too far, too low, and disappeared without a trace but a short-lived three-petalled hole in the snow.

Noel and Blanche were in a window, flashing sunrays off cutlery to attract the helicopter's attention. Lois continued to play the piano.

Ropes, a ladder, a life-buoy dangled uselessly against the glass.

Noel gesticulated.

They've seen us, Blanche said.

The rescuers were sending down a scan.

Sounds like they're having a party down there, Sir.

He's back, yet aware he's increasingly free to slip out, even without stirring from the bed.

The two men huddle, whispering, on the window-seat. He is surprised by the flexibility of the angle from which he can see them. Although they've been here a long time, he never saw them as well as now, or understood as clearly how peripheral they were. He knows his link to them is tenuous.

But others inhabit the room. Other presences more mobile, more distinct. More crucial.

Something bursts over him with a brilliance almost unbearably vivid. Before he surrenders to it, there is a lull when he isn't sure, when he has time to wonder. Is the power back on? Or is this death?